Multiplication - Easy

William S. Rogers III

iUniverse, Inc.
Bloomington

MULTIPLICATION - EASY

iUniverse books may be ordered through booksellers or by contacting:

iUniverse
1663 Liberty Drive
Bloomington, IN 47403
www.iuniverse.com
1-800-Authors (1-800-288-4677)

ISBN: 978-1-4759-8199-5 (sc)
ISBN: 978-1-4759-8200-8 (ebk)

Printed in the United States of America

iUniverse rev. date: 03/11/2013

CORRELATIONS

Dear Consumer,

Congratulations! You have just purchased a one of a kind puzzle that is geared towards education while also having fun. I have worked diligently to create a style of puzzle that is different from the rest and that would stand out easily above all the others. Correlations is a puzzle that is educational and equipped to enhance the minds of others. This style of puzzle originated out of the thought of making math fun. I wanted to create a puzzle that would help people learn or re-learn the basic math concepts and create different levels in which people could try to conquer. Correlations is suitable for all ages of people whether young or old. This puzzle can be formatted for those who want to take it easy and for those who like a little challenge.

Correlations is like an enhanced mathematical word search. I have enjoyed bringing this new style of puzzle to the market, and I hope you enjoy doing this puzzle as much as I have enjoyed creating it. Nothing is too hard to do if you just set your mind to it. Correlations is going to challenge you when it comes to math and searching for the words within the puzzle. Congratulations once again, and I hope you have a blast on your Correlations journey!

William S. Rogers III

How to Solve Correlations

- The puzzles consist of a 7x7 grid
- Solve the math within the box and try to figure out what letters go where
- You do this by knowing where each letter falls in the alphabet (EX: A=1, K=11, P=16, T=20)
- EX: To find the letter G you would look for 7X1. This comes out to equal 7=G
- Once you figure this out you have to find the words within the puzzle
- EX: GREEK – the words are not all straight or diagonal. As long as the G is touching the R box, the R is touching the E box, the E is touching the E box, and the E is touching the K box then the word is found within the puzzle
- The letters within the puzzles are only used once (**NO ONE LETTER OR BOX CAN BE USED TWICE**)
- All the boxes within the puzzle are not to be filled
- (1) (2) (3) (4) – These are used to identify the words on the Answer Sheets

Take this 7 X 7-square example on this page

2X3	2X1	3X6=R (3)	9X2=R (1)	2X10	4X2	3X4=L (4)
2X3=F (3)	5X1=E (3)	5X1=E (1)	3X5	7X3	2X10=T (4)	5X1=E (4)
2X10=T (1)	19X1=S (3)	2X6=L (1)	8X3	4X5=T (4)	3X3	2X10
5X1=E (1)	1X1=A (1)	2X7=N (3)	2X7	2X8	5X1=E (4)	2X4
3X4	3X3	1X1=A (3)	11X2	3X3	4X4	2X9=R (4)
15X1	2X9=R (3)	6X2	2X2	3X3=I (2)	3X5=O (2)	19X1=S (4)
2X10=T (3)	2X1	2X3	13X1=M (2)	13X1=M (2)	4X5=T (2)	3X1=C (2)

WORDS

1. RELATE (18, 5, 12, 1, 20, 5)
2. COMMIT (3, 15, 13, 13, 9, 20)
3. TRANSFER (20, 18, 1, 14, 19, 6, 5, 18)
4. LETTERS (12, 5, 20, 20, 5, 18, 19)

To start, look for a word that have letters that are not in the other words. The word TRANSFER; locate the letter T first by looking for 2 numbers that equal 20. T is the 20th letter in the alphabet. There are a lot of multiplication factors that come out to equal 20, but only 2X10 in the lower left hand corner is the only one that has an R multiple connected to it. Next, the R is located with the box 2X9. The letter A is diagonal from this box. There are 2 boxes after the A is found that holds an N in it. When this arises, you have to plan ahead and look for the next letter which would be the letter S. The only logical move to make after planning ahead is the 2X7=N box that is directly above the A box. From there on, the F is found diagonal from the S and then the E is found with 5X1. The last thing with trying to find the word TRANSFER is locating the R which is diagonal from the E box with 3X6. The word TRANSFER is now found within the puzzle.

If one discovers that a word is too hard to find, locate part of the word within the puzzle first, stop, and search for a new word. This is the procedure that was used in order to find the word TRANSFER. Keep in mind the Elimination Process (finding a word and not being able to reuse the same boxes over) helps a lot when situations like this arises within the puzzle. There is no guess work that needs to be done when it comes to these puzzles. All you have to do is solve the math, plan ahead, look at the surrounding boxes, and figure out where the words are within the puzzle. Use these tips in order to continue finding the rest of the words within the puzzle

Additional Tips

- Try to solve the math within the box to find the words within the puzzle
- Try and look for letters that are not in other words
- In puzzles that have similar letters within words, try and find the letters that are the same (It sometimes help to look for a word backwards, starting with the last letter in the word)
- Remember, you can only use a box once; so try and plan ahead

EASY

2X4	10X2	19X1	9X2	2X2	14X1	5X1
3X3	3X6	12X2	3X4	5X3	4X5	1X1
13X1	5X1	19X1	8X2	2X7	2X3	4X5
6X4	7X1	2X6	7X3	3X3	19X1	1X1
2X3	3X4	2X7	19X1	1X1	3X5	8X2
2X9	2X7	5X1	3X3	2X11	4X4	3X2
19X1	2X10	5X1	2X11	3X5	10X2	2X2

WORDS

1. SAVINGS
2. TELLERS
3. POINT
4. OVENS

EASY

3X3	12X2	3X2	19X1	10X2	2X1	3X4
14X1	2X7	2X8	3X5	10X1	2X7	2X5
2X7	4X3	7X1	5X3	6X3	5X1	10X2
2X2	1X1	19X1	5X1	2X9	4X4	3X2
5X5	3X4	11X1	2X11	5X1	2X2	5X3
4X6	1X1	3X5	5X1	7X3	7X1	19X1
10X2	2X2	1X1	2X10	4X5	2X8	9X2

WORDS

1. VEGAN
2. GEEKS
3. NERDS
4. TODAY

EASY

2X3	4X4	5X4	2X7	7X1	12X2	3X3
17X1	3X2	3X1	11X1	3X3	5X3	3X1
5X2	1X1	2X7	2X10	6X3	7X3	2X1
2X2	12X2	3X5	4X4	19X1	10X2	3X6
5X5	6X3	7X1	23X1	3X4	19X1	5X1
11X2	11X1	4X5	3X3	1X1	2X4	2X11
3X2	7X1	2X7	3X6	3X3	5X1	10X2

WORDS

1. SHIRT
2. KNOWING
3. ACTING
4. REVEAL

EASY

2X2	11X2	3X4	5X5	3X6	10X2	19X1
2X8	7X3	2X1	5X1	1X1	14X1	2X6
7X3	19X1	7X1	2X6	19X1	8X3	19X1
11X1	2X1	2X8	2X2	1X1	5X1	11X1
5X3	6X4	3X3	2X4	19X1	13X1	3X5
2X9	3X1	9X1	3X4	3X5	3X5	10X2
3X5	4X4	5X1	3X2	13X1	11X2	2X6

WORDS

1. HOMES
2. SPICE
3. RELAX
4. LOOKS

EASY

1X2	2X7	2X2	11X2	3X4	5X1	19X1
7X1	1X1	2X4	4X4	11X1	2X4	2X2
17X1	2X8	13X1	3X2	3X5	11X1	3X5
1X1	5X5	3X5	2X7	5X1	5X1	3X1
3X2	4X4	3X4	23X1	2X11	2X11	10X2
5X5	2X1	5X1	2X2	5X1	5X1	3X3
13X1	17X1	2X8	2X6	3X3	4X4	5X5

WORDS

1. WOMAN
2. EVENLY
3. BELIEVE
4. SHOCK

EASY

14X1	2X2	3X4	3X2	4X4	5X5	10X2
19X1	2X1	2X4	3X5	3X5	17X1	19X1
3X3	2X3	2X11	2X2	4X4	19X1	2X6
2X9	3X1	5X1	5X1	1X1	5X1	10X2
12X2	2X2	2X9	1X1	2X2	2X8	3X6
5X1	2X1	5X5	4X4	13X1	4X3	2X2
2X1	5X1	3X4	10X2	19X1	5X5	4X4

WORDS

1. LOVED
2. PAPER
3. MAYBE
4. DRESS

EASY

2X1	10X2	19X1	5X1	3X6	3X3	3X4
3X5	4X4	2X4	10X2	2X2	4X3	12X2
3X8	2X10	7X1	2X9	5X1	7X2	7X3
1X1	3X5	5X5	3X4	1X1	10X2	2X9
3X6	5X1	13X1	4X4	5X4	2X7	11X1
3X2	4X1	12X2	3X3	1X1	2X7	19X1
3X5	1X1	2X9	3X7	3X3	2X7	19X1

WORDS

1. SNAPLE
2. GRANT
3. RUINS
4. MOTHER

EASY

2X2	13X2	10X2	2X9	2X3	3X3	4X4
6X4	1X2	3X5	4X3	4X5	12X2	8X2
9X2	2X10	19X1	3X1	3X6	7X1	2X7
11X1	2X4	5X1	2X7	19X1	5X1	2X2
7X1	19X1	2X7	3X5	4X2	7X2	2X11
1X1	3X3	4X4	2X7	3X5	3X1	3X3
4X5	2X9	3X2	3X4	5X5	7X1	10X2

WORDS

1. SPONSOR
2. CONNECT
3. RIGHT
4. GIVEN

EASY

11X1	2X2	3X4	3X1	5X1	5X3	6X4
10X2	19X1	3X3	5X1	3X1	1X1	3X5
4X4	5X5	3X3	2X11	5X1	2X9	19X1
5X3	2X7	1X1	2X9	2X1	2X6	5X1
3X4	7X1	2X7	5X1	5X1	4X4	5X4
19X1	17X1	19X1	3X3	2X6	13X1	4X6
2X8	3X3	9X1	19X1	11X1	2X1	3X5

WORDS

1. NIECE
2. SERVICE
3. MELROSE
4. KINGS

EASY

2X1	2X7	3X4	5X1	4X4	3X5	10X2
5X1	19X1	2X10	1X1	3X1	2X10	3X4
2X2	3X4	3X3	5X3	3X7	3X3	5X1
6X4	19X1	5X1	2X7	12X2	3X2	3X3
5X1	2X5	4X5	3X3	3X2	4X4	3X2
11X1	17X1	1X1	2X9	13X1	3X5	2X8
4X4	3X2	10X2	3X5	2X2	19X1	17X1

WORDS

1. DENTIST
2. OFFICE
3. ORAJEL
4. MINUTE

EASY

3X3	2X7	2X9	3X3	10X2	19X1	2X1
2X5	5X1	4X4	2X6	4X4	7X1	13X1
1X1	7X1	5X1	2X8	3X2	3X5	19X1
5X5	3X3	3X6	3X4	6X4	2X2	10X2
3X2	1X1	2X10	2X7	1X1	4X4	5X1
3X3	2X4	1X1	4X2	3X7	3X4	2X8
3X1	2X6	2X1	3X7	17X1	3X1	2X2

WORDS

1. AUNTIE
2. CHARGER
3. MODEL
4. QUALIFY

EASY

11X1	3X2	2X10	3X4	2X7	2X5	3X6
3X3	1X1	2X9	2X2	1X1	5X5	2X9
3X4	10X2	3X3	2X11	1X1	3X1	2X7
2X2	4X5	5X1	5X1	1X1	6X4	19X1
17X1	3X8	7X1	2X9	2X7	3X3	4X6
11X1	3X1	1X1	2X2	3X5	2X6	2X8
2X9	3X4	4X4	3X5	2X7	2X2	5X5

WORDS

1. DODGE
2. CARAVAN
3. ONLINE
4. FRIDAY

EASY

1X1	2X3	12X2	3X4	19X1	4X5	4X4
5X5	2X8	3X6	10X2	1X1	17X1	2X8
4X3	2X2	1X1	13X1	2X7	5X5	2X2
1X1	3X2	19X1	2X2	1X1	5X1	5X1
19X1	3X4	2X2	5X1	3X3	2X7	2X10
5X3	3X3	1X1	2X6	13X1	3X5	3X3
12X2	4X3	3X1	10X2	3X8	2X5	9X2

WORDS

1. STANDARD
2. MEDICAL
3. TEAMS
4. JOINED

EASY

2X2	12X2	3X3	2X4	10X2	19X1	11X1
17X1	2X4	10X2	4X5	19X1	3X3	2X4
4X4	3X3	2X7	3X7	23X1	4X5	3X2
12X2	3X6	13X1	2X2	2X9	3X5	5X5
1X1	3X3	2X7	13X1	3X6	5X5	10X2
19X1	5X1	3X4	3X5	7X1	1X1	3X2
5X4	4X6	3X2	3X1	4X4	2X8	2X1

WORDS

1. INDUSTRY
2. GROWTH
3. LEARN
4. COMMIT

EASY

19X1	2X8	3X3	10X2	1X1	2X4	4X2
5X5	4X3	17X1	19X1	13X1	19X1	17X1
7X1	2X8	5X1	23X1	8X3	3X3	4X4
5X5	5X4	3X3	2X7	3X5	2X8	3X4
1X1	2X9	3X6	2X6	2X11	2X4	2X11
12X2	5X1	11X1	3X3	13X1	5X1	13X2
3X3	4X1	23X1	5X1	2X9	10X2	19X1

WORDS

1. VIEWER
2. SWIRL
3. PHONE
4. SILVER

EASY

23X1	5X5	4X2	6X2	2X2	5X1	2X2
10X2	11X1	3X4	1X1	4X4	3X3	2X9
5X4	6X3	19X1	2X8	19X1	1X1	3X5
3X2	2X7	2X10	4X2	17X1	3X4	13X1
19X1	3X3	3X5	2X2	2X1	3X5	4X4
3X3	2X7	4X5	3X7	2X7	6X4	4X2
8X3	2X1	7X1	2X10	11X1	17X1	5X1

WORDS

1. BUTTON
2. DIAMOND
3. LASTING
4. EXPLORE

EASY

11X1	2X3	10X2	3X2	4X4	6X4	7X1
17X1	8X3	3X5	2X2	2X9	3X5	3X3
19X1	2X7	4X4	19X1	1X1	4X4	3X4
3X2	10X2	3X7	3X3	3X6	5X1	3X3
2X11	19X1	23X1	2X8	4X5	1X1	23X1
2X2	3X2	5X1	5X1	2X4	4X4	2X10
17X1	3X4	1X1	3X1	4X4	6X4	5X5

WORDS

1. PEACH
2. PERSON
3. SUITE
4. TAILOR

EASY

11X1	2X3	10X2	19X1	3X2	4X4	3X1
5X5	5X1	3X6	17X1	3X1	2X4	19X1
23X1	5X5	2X1	2X9	3X5	5X1	1X1
2X2	5X1	5X1	13X1	3X5	3X3	5X1
3X4	3X5	3X3	2X6	23X1	19X1	11X1
23X1	4X4	2X7	3X3	13X1	4X5	19X1
5X5	2X6	2X8	7X1	3X4	10X2	2X7

WORDS

1. SMILE
2. COMING
3. EYEBROW
4. CHEEKS

EASY

19X1	2X2	10X2	3X4	5X5	5X3	11X1
13X1	3X7	17X1	3X4	2X8	4X4	4X3
23X1	3X6	4X5	19X1	3X4	2X10	3X1
5X5	19X1	4X4	3X7	3X5	3X5	3X2
3X3	1X1	13X1	2X9	3X5	13X1	1X1
13X2	4X3	10X2	3X3	3X2	2X4	4X5
2X8	5X5	19X1	5X1	3X5	2X9	19X1

WORDS

1. SURPRISE
2. COMFORT
3. PLUMS
4. SHOOT

EASY

23X1	3X3	1X1	4X4	5X4	10X2	19X1
11X1	10X2	3X2	2X2	4X3	13X1	12X2
3X2	2X2	13X1	4X5	1X1	5X5	1X1
12X2	3X6	2X9	3X3	3X3	4X6	13X1
11X1	5X1	3X5	4X5	2X7	19X1	11X1
17X1	2X7	2X8	3X4	5X1	5X1	3X1
1X1	2X4	8X3	3X1	2X6	3X3	13X2

WORDS

1. NOTES
2. MAINE
3. ADMIRE
4. CLICK

EASY

3X2	19X1	10X2	2X7	2X2	4X5	7X1
4X4	12X2	11X1	13X2	1X1	2X7	19X1
11X1	17X1	23X1	1X1	2X4	3X3	3X4
3X2	4X3	19X1	5X3	3X4	2X10	11X1
2X2	5X1	2X1	12X2	2X7	3X5	3X4
3X5	23X1	19X1	3X5	3X5	3X3	2X8
3X4	5X5	19X1	4X4	2X4	19X1	2X1

WORDS

1. BOSSES
2. THANKS
3. INLAW
4. HOOKING

EASY

1X1	12X2	13X2	23X1	1X1	3X4	5X5
4X5	3X6	3X1	5X5	19X1	2X6	17X1
3X3	2X1	5X1	2X4	13X1	3X3	4X2
10X2	19X1	3X2	3X7	3X5	11X1	4X5
4X4	4X5	11X1	2X7	2X7	5X1	5X5
11X1	17X1	5X1	23X1	5X1	2X9	4X6
13X2	2X1	19X1	5X5	4X5	4X3	19X1

WORDS

1. MONKEY
2. CHUNK
3. SWEET
4. LAWYER

EASY

11X1	10X2	2X2	5X1	19X1	2X3	4X4
5X4	2X7	5X5	11X1	5X1	23X1	12X2
7X1	3X4	3X3	2X8	3X1	9X2	19X1
17X1	19X1	3X4	2X2	23X1	3X1	2X8
3X2	4X5	5X1	2X6	3X5	3X7	2X9
5X5	10X2	19X1	3X3	19X1	3X1	3X5
1X1	3X2	2X1	19X1	5X1	3X1	4X4

WORDS

1. CODES
2. BILLING
3. PROCESS
4. SUCCEED

EASY

2X2	2X11	5X1	12X2	19X1	3X2	4X4
5X4	5X5	5X1	2X9	3X7	11X1	10X2
2X3	3X6	5X1	19X1	4X4	6X4	4X5
13X2	2X1	2X7	3X6	3X7	2X9	4X3
19X1	17X1	2X1	3X3	1X1	11X1	5X1
3X3	2X2	2X9	3X5	3X5	3X1	3X4
5X1	17X1	2X1	2X8	3X6	1X1	4X5

WORDS

1. INSURE
2. CAREER
3. BROOK
4. ALERT

EASY

2X11	3X3	4X4	5X1	2X4	5X5	10X2
19X1	11X1	2X2	17X1	7X1	3X1	4X2
2X2	3X2	2X9	2X7	1X1	5X1	2X4
4X4	5X5	3X5	5X1	3X3	19X1	3X2
2X7	3X7	11X1	3X3	2X11	2X6	3X6
5X1	19X1	2X9	3X5	3X4	3X4	4X1
19X1	5X1	2X10	17X1	13X1	23X1	5X5

WORDS

1. SKILLS
2. MOVING
3. REACHED
4. FOURTEEN

EASY

4X4	12X2	3X3	4X3	10X2	3X4	5X5
13X2	2X2	4X5	2X1	1X1	11X1	19X1
2X8	5X5	4X2	3X6	3X7	17X1	2X11
23X1	2X7	7X1	5X1	3X1	3X1	4X3
3X7	2X7	3X2	2X2	11X1	2X10	3X3
2X9	1X1	3X3	5X1	5X1	2X4	19X1
17X1	19X1	2X2	1X1	4X5	4X5	6X4

WORDS

1. DEATH
2. TRUCK
3. NURSING
4. DEFECT

EASY

2X2	13X2	5X5	4X3	3X2	12X2	1X1
2X10	3X4	2X7	7X1	2X7	3X7	6X2
17X1	19X1	3X6	3X3	2X7	7X1	2X9
3X4	1X1	19X1	3X5	3X6	3X5	7X1
5X1	1X1	2X9	13X1	3X6	2X4	5X1
4X2	3X4	3X5	2X10	3X7	5X3	3X3
11X1	2X11	23X1	3X1	19X1	23X1	1X1

WORDS

1. HUMOR
2. LEASING
3. STRONG
4. CORAL

EASY

2X10	1X1	13X1	1X1	3X4	5X5	3X6
5X5	4X2	2X9	19X1	19X1	3X1	3X3
2X9	12X2	3X2	4X5	3X3	2X7	5X1
13X2	2X6	5X1	1X1	2X10	2X2	3X2
4X3	2X1	3X4	5X1	19X1	2X2	5X1
2X7	4X4	2X9	3X7	3X6	19X1	3X7
13X2	2X11	2X5	3X5	2X8	23X1	5X5

WORDS

1. REEFS
2. JUSTICE
3. PROPS
4. INSTALL

EASY

2X11	23X1	19X1	3X3	4X5	5X3	6X4
2X1	12X2	5X1	11X1	5X1	2X2	5X2
17X1	3X8	3X6	19X1	3X2	3X4	2X8
3X5	3X4	3X5	1X1	7X1	1X1	23X1
2X10	23X1	2X1	7X1	4X4	1X1	2X5
1X1	2X2	3X3	19X1	19X1	3X4	5X5
13X2	23X1	2X2	3X8	2X6	19X1	2X1

WORDS

1. BOXES
2. SPARKS
3. WALLS
4. WIGGLE

EASY

2X8	11X1	2X1	13X2	7X1	19X1	2X8
3X6	3X5	5X5	2X7	4X5	5X1	5X4
4X2	19X1	1X1	2X10	2X9	2X11	2X1
5X1	2X4	19X1	7X1	23X1	1X1	2X3
17X1	3X1	3X3	2X7	2X6	13X1	1X1
2X9	3X6	3X5	2X1	2X2	5X1	3X1
3X7	3X1	13X2	2X11	4X6	3X7	2X10

WORDS

1. POSSIBLE
2. CONDUCT
3. TRAMA
4. CHANGE

EASY

2X11	3X3	23X1	5X5	2X9	3X7	10X2
19X1	2X2	3X4	5X1	4X5	3X3	1X1
2X8	7X1	3X3	2X3	13X1	2X7	5X1
3X5	3X7	2X8	9X2	2X2	2X1	1X1
3X3	10X2	11X2	4X6	2X10	3X1	2X2
17X1	19X1	5X1	13X1	5X1	5X1	3X3
12X2	13X2	4X5	4X3	1X1	3X6	4X4

WORDS

1. REMIND
2. TEXTED
3. AMERICA
4. BEAUTY

EASY

1X1	7X1	2X3	3X7	5X1	3X4	4X5
5X3	3X6	2X7	17X1	19X1	2X8	2X1
5X1	7X1	3X3	3X6	1X1	5X1	2X2
11X1	12X2	13X1	2X10	5X1	5X1	23X1
23X1	4X6	3X3	5X1	4X4	2X11	3X7
3X8	1X1	13X2	2X2	3X7	3X3	19X1
2X7	2X8	3X3	3X7	2X7	2X9	3X2

WORDS

1. PURSUE
2. MEDIA
3. UNIVERSE
4. BEATING

EASY

2X3	3X5	10X2	19X1	13X2	12X2	4X3
4X5	5X5	5X1	19X1	17X1	2X8	2X2
3X2	13X1	2X7	19X1	13X1	3X3	2X1
4X4	19X1	5X1	5X1	5X1	19X1	5X4
3X3	3X7	2X9	4X4	3X4	5X1	5X1
12X2	11X2	1X1	3X3	3X8	2X8	1X1
11X1	23X1	19X1	3X1	13X1	19X1	5X1

WORDS

1. EXPENSE
2. SIMPLE
3. CAUSES
4. DISEASE

EASY

12X2	23X1	3X2	1X1	2X2	11X1	3X5
2X9	3X3	3X4	5X1	3X7	8X2	10X2
5X1	7X1	19X1	3X5	2X5	5X1	13X2
2X7	23X1	5X1	23X1	1X1	3X2	3X3
4X4	4X3	2X9	3X3	2X10	7X1	19X1
2X8	3X3	9X2	3X7	2X7	5X1	11X2
23X1	4X2	19X1	1X1	3X4	3X7	3X6

WORDS

1. FEATURE
2. FLOWING
3. SALES
4. DESIGN

EASY

2X2	13X1	23X1	2X11	2X9	3X3	2X8
2X10	4X3	3X5	3X3	3X2	11X2	23X1
12X2	5X5	2X10	3X6	5X3	2X2	2X10
3X1	5X1	2X4	5X1	5X1	3X7	19X1
17X1	5X1	1X1	2X11	2X9	2X8	2X1
3X6	7X1	13X2	5X1	3X4	3X3	3X8
3X7	2X6	2X7	1X1	7X1	2X7	5X5

WORDS

1. PLAZA
2. REVENGE
3. MOTHER
4. TUBING

EASY

11X1	2X1	1X1	3X5	3X2	5X5	3X4
4X4	10X2	23X1	5X1	2X2	19X1	5X5
3X2	12X2	7X1	2X2	5X1	5X1	5X1
3X8	3X6	3X3	3X6	13X1	2X9	19X1
4X1	2X7	7X1	5X1	1X1	3X5	2X2
13X2	3X1	3X3	2X4	4X4	11X1	3X1
2X11	4X5	3X1	2X4	4X5	19X1	1X1

WORDS

1. THEMES
2. GRAPHIC
3. SCORES
4. FEEDING

EASY

2X11	3X3	12X2	19X1	4X3	5X5	23X1
3X3	12X2	10X2	2X7	7X1	4X5	4X4
4X3	13X2	7X1	2X9	3X3	3X7	5X1
2X7	3X8	1X1	1X1	5X1	5X1	3X6
5X4	7X1	3X6	3X2	2X6	3X7	12X2
11X1	13X1	12X2	3X3	5X1	3X5	2X2
4X2	3X3	3X4	23X1	2X4	19X1	2X6

WORDS

1. FEUDS
2. ARGUE
3. WHOLE
4. GRAIN

EASY

5X5	4X3	2X9	12X2	3X4	13X2	2X11
23X1	3X3	2X2	3X6	2X6	4X6	4X3
2X10	2X7	3X4	5X1	1X1	5X1	19X1
7X1	5X1	13X1	7X1	5X1	3X1	2X4
19X1	2X4	3X8	3X6	7X1	2X4	19X1
2X8	3X3	4X1	3X7	1X1	2X2	17X1
3X4	12X2	23X1	2X5	3X6	5X5	4X4

WORDS

1. CHARMED
2. JUGGLE
3. SHELL
4. EARRING

EASY

3X3	3X1	12X2	2X2	2X4	5X5	2X11
23X1	17X1	2X8	3X1	3X4	5X3	19X1
11X1	19X1	2X9	4X5	1X1	7X1	13X1
2X11	3X1	2X10	5X1	2X7	3X5	3X1
4X4	5X1	1X1	4X5	3X3	3X2	2X7
2X8	19X1	5X1	7X1	1X1	19X1	17X1
13X1	2X4	5X5	4X5	2X2	4X4	3X7

WORDS

1. STAGING
2. UPDATE
3. COACH
4. SECRET

EASY

2X2	13X2	2X10	12X2	2X2	10X2	19X1
17X1	1X1	2X8	5X1	3X3	4X2	6X4
5X3	11X1	2X6	23X1	2X2	2X2	3X6
2X8	2X9	3X5	2X7	2X9	5X1	2X7
3X1	7X1	5X1	3X1	3X5	1X1	3X6
2X3	12X2	23X1	7X1	2X4	3X7	5X1
2X11	11X1	2X9	5X1	2X10	3X1	2X4

WORDS

1. GENDER
2. CHOCOLATE
3. RETURN
4. HEARD

EASY

11X1	2X1	13X2	5X1	2X11	23X1	3X4
3X1	19X1	2X6	4X6	7X1	19X1	12X1
2X1	3X4	17X1	2X1	2X8	5X1	3X6
3X7	5X5	6X2	2X1	3X7	2X11	2X9
12X2	13X1	3X7	3X4	3X3	5X1	3X1
4X5	4X3	2X6	2X1	18X1	2X4	5X3
13X2	5X5	5X1	7X1	1X1	23X1	1X1

WORDS

1. CLUBS
2. BUBBLE
3. CHILL
4. LEVERAGE

EASY

23X1	12X2	3X4	5X3	19X1	2X10	3X4
4X5	5X5	3X3	2X7	3X3	6X3	12X2
13X2	23X1	7X1	14X1	2X4	2X6	23X1
2X2	3X5	2X2	19X1	7X1	3X3	7X1
5X1	2X9	2X4	3X7	3X2	2X7	6X3
11X2	3X5	19X1	2X7	3X4	11X1	13X1
19X1	3X2	23X1	4X5	5X5	2X1	6X1

WORDS

1. FILING
2. SHOWING
3. BLUSH
4. DROWN

EASY

2X3	3X3	13X1	12X2	17X1	1X1	3X3
19X1	3X5	2X7	3X5	3X6	7X1	5X1
13X2	23X1	12X2	19X1	19X1	3X3	4X4
5X2	11X1	4X5	5X1	19X1	5X1	23X1
17X1	3X4	19X1	17X1	2X8	2X4	5X1
19X1	2X8	5X5	1X1	3X7	2X9	19X1
2X6	3X4	4X5	5X1	1X1	3X3	1X1

WORDS

1. SQUARE
2. MOSTLY
3. TEASE
4. ASHES

EASY

23X1	2X2	12X2	2X10	3X3	5X5	5X3
3X2	4X3	2X2	3X5	4X4	19X1	3X6
17X1	7X1	3X4	3X6	2X9	3X3	19X1
3X4	12X2	3X5	3X3	3X5	19X1	13X2
2X2	3X1	2X2	2X6	23X1	13X1	2X11
2X4	4X6	2X10	3X4	5X1	5X1	3X8
17X1	4X5	5X5	1X1	3X2	12X2	13X1

WORDS

1. SWEAT
2. DRILL
3. COLORS
4. MEMOIR

EASY

13X2	2X2	4X3	5X5	3X5	2X11	17X1
2X8	3X1	3X3	5X2	5X1	3X5	19X1
2X10	13X1	11X1	7X1	4X5	2X7	4X3
13X2	23X1	1X1	2X10	3X3	2X7	1X1
13X1	2X9	8X3	1X1	3X3	5X1	7X1
4X5	19X1	4X4	2X9	4X5	4X6	2X2
3X7	23X1	2X2	8X1	2X9	2X11	23X1

WORDS

1. TATTOO
2. SPRING
3. IMAGINE
4. DEALS

EASY

5X3	4X6	2X8	11X2	2X4	7X1	19X1
11X1	13X1	13X2	1X1	2X6	13X1	3X3
3X4	5X5	3X7	2X2	5X5	5X1	5X1
23X1	7X1	5X5	5X1	2X9	1X1	2X7
2X7	7X1	5X1	5X1	5X1	2X10	2X6
1X1	3X3	2X2	2X7	2X7	2X1	5X1
2X3	2X6	12X2	1X1	5X1	3X6	13X2

WORDS

1. NEEDLE
2. GENERAL
3. READING
4. PAYMENT

EASY

3X4	11X2	13X1	2X2	19X1	2X10	4X3
4X4	5X5	2X7	2X7	3X7	3X5	1X1
12X2	4X1	3X5	2X10	3X6	2X2	13X1
23X1	3X4	3X3	4X5	5X1	11X1	19X1
2X11	3X5	19X1	3X3	3X1	3X1	17X1
2X8	3X6	5X1	5X1	3X3	5X1	3X1
5X1	7X1	3X6	3X3	2X8	2X4	4X3

WORDS

1. RECIPE
2. NOTICE
3. AMOUNT
4. WORRIES

EASY

23X1	3X1	4X4	5X3	5X5	2X7	11X2
11X1	13X1	2X4	1X1	2X7	7X1	5X1
2X4	3X1	2X2	3X1	1X1	5X1	3X4
19X1	2X8	5X1	1X1	2X9	3X4	5X1
3X6	3X5	2X8	2X11	3X3	3X1	4X5
4X6	5X5	3X3	2X10	5X1	2X10	23X1
2X11	2X8	3X6	19X1	1X1	2X6	3X7

WORDS

1. SETTLE
2. CAPITAL
3. DEVICE
4. CHANNEL

EASY

12X2	13X1	2X2	1X1	19X1	1X1	17X1
3X2	5X5	5X3	3X3	2X8	2X10	2X11
13X1	19X1	2X9	11X1	1X1	3X8	11X2
2X8	5X1	1X1	19X1	4X5	3X4	5X1
17X1	3X7	3X4	7X1	5X1	3X5	4X4
3X2	12X2	5X1	1X1	3X1	19X1	13X2
4X6	5X5	5X3	2X11	11X1	4X3	4X1

WORDS

1. LOCALS
2. STATES
3. VEGAS
4. EXPIRE

EASY

4X4	13X2	2X2	3X6	5X5	11X1	7X1
2X2	3X2	5X1	6X3	4X5	8X2	8X3
19X1	2X6	3X1	1X1	5X1	7X1	4X5
2X10	3X4	2X1	2X9	3X4	2X2	11X2
13X1	1X1	5X1	3X7	3X5	13X2	2X7
3X7	2X2	7X1	2X7	1X1	2X1	12X2
3X4	5X4	5X3	2X6	3X1	2X4	1X1

WORDS

1. GLOBAL
2. CRUNCH
3. DEBATED
4. GALLERY

EASY

2X10	2X2	3X1	12X2	4X4	5X3	6X2
4X2	1X1	3X3	2X6	11X2	13X1	2X8
9X2	2X7	1X1	2X2	2X2	4X6	5X1
19X1	3X1	7X1	2X7	2X6	19X1	17X1
2X2	3X3	2X1	3X7	5X1	2X7	2X6
3X7	7X1	3X2	23X1	3X5	2X1	3X4
2X11	2X10	3X1	11X2	2X9	3X5	2X1

WORDS

1. WELDING
2. BOUND
3. FICAL
4. ROLLS

EASY

11X1	2X3	3X3	2X9	23X1	13X1	13X2
3X3	5X4	5X1	3X5	5X5	5X1	17X1
7X1	2X10	2X4	11X1	2X9	19X1	3X6
5X1	19X1	19X1	2X1	3X6	3X3	2X5
4X4	4X3	3X3	5X1	13X2	2X7	7X1
2X11	23X1	2X6	7X1	5X1	3X6	23X1
2X1	2X3	4X4	3X1	1X1	2X8	3X6

WORDS

1. BRING
2. CLERK
3. REGISTER
4. SHOWER

EASY

3X5	5X5	5X1	12X2	3X3	3X3	13X2
13X1	1X1	17X1	2X7	1X1	1X1	7X1
19X1	3X6	2X2	5X1	3X4	13X1	2X9
5X5	4X5	2X6	3X2	5X5	3X5	3X2
11X2	3X4	3X3	3X1	13X2	5X1	4X6
3X4	5X1	1X1	5X1	3X3	7X1	9X2
23X1	2X11	2X9	4X5	2X9	2X1	1X1

WORDS

1. MAINLY
2. GEORGIA
3. EARLIER
4. RECALL

EASY

12X2	2X7	5X1	13X1	2X2	5X5	5X3
5X1	2X2	4X5	13X1	3X7	19X1	17X1
2X11	7X1	3X3	13X1	5X1	1X1	2X8
2X2	23X1	2X1	2X7	3X3	13X1	2X7
5X1	2X7	3X8	7X1	2X9	3X3	3X7
4X6	1X1	2X9	3X5	3X4	2X10	3X6
23X1	4X4	3X1	2X11	2X1	4X5	1X1

WORDS

1. VENTING
2. TRIMMED
3. CAROLINA
4. TRUMP

EASY

2X1	11X2	19X1	13X2	3X3	4X1	5X4
2X11	17X1	3X3	5X1	3X3	3X3	2X2
3X7	1X1	5X1	4X4	2X8	2X2	2X7
11X2	3X4	2X10	13X2	3X3	3X5	7X1
4X6	11X1	5X5	3X1	3X5	2X2	5X3
3X6	8X2	3X3	19X1	7X1	8X3	9X2
2X11	1X1	4X4	2X2	2X2	1X1	23X1

WORDS

1. GOODIES
2. SPARKLE
3. ADDICT
4. DIPPING

EASY

1X1	12X2	2X9	13X2	7X1	13X1	3X7
2X7	5X1	5X3	1X1	5X1	19X1	17X1
7X1	4X3	2X2	2X7	3X3	2X2	4X4
2X10	5X5	3X5	7X1	2X7	3X6	5X1
2X11	13X1	2X9	1X1	1X1	4X5	2X2
17X1	3X3	23X1	3X5	2X4	8X3	8X2
3X1	4X5	5X5	3X4	7X1	3X7	17X1

WORDS

1. DRAGON
2. WANTED
3. GLORY
4. GEARED

EASY

2X3	12X2	4X5	19X1	5X5	3X5	2X10
3X3	4X1	13X2	2X4	3X3	3X2	3X7
1X1	3X6	2X2	5X1	3X2	11X2	7X1
2X2	1X1	5X1	2X7	5X1	2X7	11X1
13X2	12X2	2X10	3X6	4X6	3X3	5X3
5X5	2X8	19X1	3X4	13X1	19X1	4X5
7X1	3X3	1X1	3X7	5X1	2X9	5X1

WORDS

1. OFFEND
2. MUSTARD
3. ALERTING
4. SHEER

EASY

2X3	4X3	5X5	2X8	2X2	9X2	3X1
12X2	7X2	3X1	3X7	5X1	5X1	19X1
13X2	2X2	2X7	11X2	4X5	2X10	11X1
19X1	3X5	3X6	1X1	2X9	19X1	2X8
3X4	5X1	2X2	3X3	3X7	7X1	2X1
2X10	2X11	2X6	3X4	3X5	5X1	2X8
23X1	2X4	4X3	4X4	3X2	5X4	5X5

WORDS

1. FLIRTED
2. GUARDS
3. PEOPLE
4. DONUTS

EASY

6X2	3X4	1X1	12X2	4X4	3X3	4X2
5X5	12X2	1X1	19X1	13X2	13X1	2X9
3X2	5X1	2X2	3X3	4X3	5X1	2X10
2X1	2X11	13X1	5X1	5X1	3X6	3X2
3X7	11X2	2X10	2X2	3X5	4X6	4X5
5X5	2X1	5X1	1X1	2X7	3X3	2X6
23X1	3X1	3X3	2X9	5X1	19X1	17X1

WORDS

1. ASPIRE
2. OATMEAL
3. LINDER
4. FREED

EASY

5X3	2X10	3X3	12X2	3X1	19X1	2X1
2X11	13X2	2X4	3X4	7X1	12X2	2X10
3X2	11X1	3X5	3X7	3X5	2X4	19X1
17X1	2X4	23X1	5X5	19X1	5X3	2X9
5X5	2X2	19X1	5X1	2X10	19X1	3X2
4X5	5X2	4X5	2X10	3X7	2X2	8X3
3X4	4X6	1X1	2X4	7X1	3X3	4X5

WORDS

1. CLOSET
2. DUSTY
3. TIGHTS
4. THOUGHT

EASY

2X11	1X1	19X1	5X1	3X6	5X5	7X1
6X3	2X2	2X4	3X3	7X1	5X1	2X2
19X1	4X1	4X5	2X7	5X1	3X7	3X5
7X1	17X1	3X5	5X1	19X1	2X1	2X2
23X1	4X5	13X2	3X7	7X1	3X5	5X1
7X3	4X3	3X5	4X4	3X5	13X1	2X1
1X1	11X2	13X1	19X1	3X5	2X10	11X1

WORDS

1. TOGETHER
2. MOUSE
3. SOMEBODY
4. TONGUE

EASY

5X1	23X1	19X1	2X11	13X2	12X2	3X4
4X4	4X6	3X5	11X1	23X1	19X1	2X10
17X1	5X1	3X3	2X9	4X3	3X5	4X4
2X8	2X6	3X4	3X6	5X5	2X9	3X6
3X7	2X11	5X1	2X4	2X10	4X5	23X1
3X1	1X1	7X1	2X9	5X1	2X9	1X1
11X2	2X6	13X2	7X1	5X1	3X2	5X5

WORDS

1. WORTH
2. LEGAL
3. SORRY
4. REGRET

EASY

13X1	11X2	2X2	19X1	3X2	5X3	5X1
1X1	3X4	1X1	3X4	2X10	2X8	4X4
7X1	19X1	17X1	2X7	5X1	3X5	5X3
5X2	2X10	7X1	3X5	2X9	2X6	4X2
12X2	2X7	5X1	13X2	19X1	2X9	19X1
13X1	3X6	3X3	19X1	3X3	3X2	5X5
4X5	2X11	23X1	7X1	2X7	19X1	17X1

WORDS

1. MASTER
2. RINGING
3. PERSONAL
4. SLOTS

EASY

1X1	12X2	13X1	4X4	2X2	5X5	4X5
3X7	5X4	19X1	17X1	7X1	2X9	4X1
2X8	1X1	2X7	5X1	3X5	2X7	5X1
4X5	13X2	3X3	3X2	3X3	4X5	19X1
19X1	2X2	3X1	2X2	11X1	1X1	3X3
2X4	23X1	3X5	3X6	1X1	3X4	3X1
11X1	17X1	3X1	5X1	2X2	3X7	3X5

WORDS

1. STANFORD
2. LADIES
3. EDUCATE
4. WORKING

EASY

2X1	3X5	19X1	3X3	11X1	3X2	3X3
4X4	3X7	2X10	3X3	4X5	13X2	4X6
5X1	7X1	2X7	4X5	2X4	5X5	7X3
8X3	2X2	2X7	5X1	19X1	9X2	17X1
5X1	2X2	3X6	3X7	3X2	3X7	4X3
4X4	12X2	13X1	5X1	17X1	2X9	2X3
19X1	2X10	11X2	2X9	2X8	4X5	4X4

WORDS

1. BUTTER
2. RUSHING
3. DEPOSIT
4. REFUND

EASY

3X4	4X4	11X1	2X7	2X8	13X2	11X2
3X4	5X5	3X3	19X1	7X1	2X9	4X5
17X1	2X4	2X10	3X5	2X2	3X5	5X1
2X8	5X1	19X1	1X1	13X1	5X1	3X3
3X4	2X4	4X3	1X1	5X1	3X6	1X1
5X5	2X11	23X1	5X5	3X1	2X4	2X10
11X1	2X8	4X6	7X3	3X1	3X3	19X1

WORDS

1. PROMOTE
2. CASHING
3. AHEAD
4. STREET

EASY

3X3	12X2	3X1	5X1	19X1	2X1	2X10
4X3	5X5	4X5	19X1	13X2	11X1	5X3
5X5	6X4	13X1	5X1	2X1	2X6	2X3
4X4	5X5	10X2	2X9	2X1	1X1	3X5
3X4	3X1	2X1	5X1	5X1	3X3	3X5
2X11	4X4	4X5	2X10	2X2	3X6	2X2
1X1	13X1	5X1	3X7	4X6	2X8	9X2

WORDS

1. TERMS
2. DIABETES
3. METER
4. BLOOD

EASY

2X10	19X1	7X1	5X1	3X3	2X2	4X4
5X4	5X5	11X2	3X3	3X5	3X4	11X2
13X2	4X5	13X1	17X1	5X1	2X4	5X1
5X1	2X10	1X1	2X10	3X6	5X1	4X5
2X3	3X1	4X3	2X7	3X4	2X10	5X1
2X8	5X1	2X2	2X9	1X1	13X1	19X1
2X11	2X10	4X5	5X1	3X4	5X5	6X4

WORDS

1. ALTERNATE
2. STEEL
3. DETECT
4. METHOD

EASY

12X2	3X3	4X4	5X5	5X3	12X2	13X2
3X7	3X4	7X2	2X10	2X4	4X5	1X1
11X1	2X1	1X1	7X1	2X7	3X5	5X1
2X8	5X1	3X3	3X7	5X1	2X7	5X1
9X2	3X4	5X5	2X10	1X1	23X1	4X5
2X11	2X2	3X7	1X1	8X3	2X10	2X1
23X1	4X6	3X6	13X1	3X2	6X2	1X1

WORDS

1. TWENTY
2. MUTUAL
3. EIGHTEEN
4. DRAFT

EASY

3X4	3X5	12X2	23X1	4X5	5X5	6X4
3X7	3X4	6X4	12X2	13X2	1X1	3X1
5X1	4X4	1X1	23X1	5X1	23X1	11X1
2X10	2X11	3X3	2X7	1X1	11X1	1X1
5X3	3X6	5X1	3X1	7X1	7X1	2X9
3X7	8X3	4X3	5X1	3X5	3X3	1X1
11X2	13X2	3X2	19X1	2X7	19X1	8X2

WORDS

1. WAGES
2. RENEW
3. SOCIAL
4. AGAIN

EASY

3X2	12X2	4X4	19X1	3X7	13X2	1X1
5X5	19X1	5X1	5X1	2X8	3X4	8X3
3X7	6X4	5X3	3X6	19X1	2X2	2X8
2X11	23X1	3X2	19X1	2X6	5X1	3X3
2X10	5X1	19X1	1X1	2X8	19X1	17X1
2X3	3X1	2X11	5X1	2X9	6X4	3X5
7X1	5X1	4X5	3X5	2X9	3X7	8X2

WORDS

1. DEPRESS
2. OVALS
3. PERFECT
4. PLUSES

EASY

3X4	2X11	3X3	5X5	4X3	12X1	19X1
3X2	3X3	5X3	3X3	3X7	3X5	17X1
2X2	4X4	2X9	4X4	2X7	3X7	5X5
11X2	2X10	19X1	7X1	13X2	13X1	4X5
19X1	3X1	2X10	5X1	1X1	1X1	3X6
1X1	3X3	11X1	2X10	7X1	23X1	5X5
3X6	2X4	3X1	7X3	4X4	12X2	13X1

WORDS

1. LIPSTICK
2. WATCH
3. OUTRAGE
4. STRING

EASY

7X3	3X3	3X6	5X1	19X1	12X2	13X1
19X1	5X1	7X1	2X9	3X4	2X4	4X4
5X5	2X9	5X1	2X2	2X10	1X1	2X11
13X2	3X7	3X8	2X10	4X5	6X3	3X7
19X1	5X1	2X1	3X5	17X1	3X1	12X2
4X6	19X1	2X2	5X1	3X2	1X1	4X4
5X3	5X5	13X2	3X3	2X1	5X4	2X11

WORDS

1. SHATTER
2. FOXES
3. ABIDE
4. BURGER

EASY

2X3	12X2	2X10	13X2	2X9	4X5	5X5
2X11	19X1	7X1	3X3	5X1	17X1	23X1
4X4	5X2	1X1	1X1	2X4	3X3	4X4
4X3	5X1	2X9	2X7	2X10	2X8	3X4
2X8	4X5	5X1	7X1	4X4	2X7	3X7
3X6	19X1	19X1	7X1	1X1	5X1	6X4
13X2	3X3	2X1	3X5	13X1	2X4	17X1

WORDS

1. SEGMENT
2. GANGS
3. HAPPIER
4. TRAIT

EASY

2X11	13X2	12X2	3X4	5X3	2X10	2X10
19X1	5X1	2X7	4X4	3X1	3X3	5X5
3X4	3X3	5X1	2X2	19X1	3X1	2X9
11X2	3X4	3X6	19X1	2X4	5X1	11X1
2X1	2X8	7X1	4X5	3X7	4X5	3X4
8X3	4X4	3X5	2X2	2X6	5X1	1X1
2X8	9X2	4X2	2X10	2X1	3X2	23X1

WORDS

1. TICKLE
2. GRIND
3. TOPLESS
4. FATHER

EASY

2X11	3X4	2X1	3X1	11X1	4X4	18X1
5X5	3X7	1X1	2X7	7X1	5X1	4X5
12X2	3X1	13X2	13X1	4X5	3X3	7X2
2X10	5X1	11X1	17X1	19X1	3X8	23X1
23X1	4X4	3X4	2X1	1X1	2X4	19X1
3X4	4X1	13X1	3X3	2X9	3X5	5X5
23X1	19X1	17X1	2X3	6X4	7X3	12X2

WORDS

1. BUCKLE
2. SHRIMP
3. REIGN
4. SMACK

EASY

2X11	5X1	2X5	4X5	5X5	12X2	13X2
19X1	2X10	3X3	5X1	5X3	4X4	3X8
9X2	2X4	2X9	3X3	1X1	13X2	12X2
5X3	11X1	2X10	3X5	5X1	19X1	17X1
11X2	5X5	1X1	3X1	3X5	19X1	3X3
4X4	2X9	3X5	3X3	13X1	1X1	2X7
13X2	2X7	2X1	19X1	4X5	6X3	8X2

WORDS

1. JERKY
2. SMOOTHIE
3. NATION
4. BRACES

EASY

2X11	2X8	3X3	10X2	19X1	17X1	4X2
4X4	19X1	1X1	12X2	13X2	2X2	5X5
3X4	5X1	2X7	4X5	19X1	5X1	3X3
3X1	2X10	2X6	2X11	5X1	5X1	4X5
3X3	19X1	5X1	3X4	7X3	2X9	3X2
3X5	1X1	11X2	23X1	2X1	3X4	23X1
4X5	2X11	23X1	3X1	3X5	2X6	7X2

WORDS

1. WRESTLE
2. BLEED
3. PANTS
4. VOICES

EASY

2X2	12X2	13X1	3X2	2X4	4X5	19X1
17X1	5X1	2X2	3X6	2X10	3X3	4X5
4X4	2X5	7X1	2X8	3X7	5X1	3X6
4X6	7X1	3X2	2X9	3X5	5X1	19X1
23X1	3X6	2X11	1X1	3X4	5X1	2X10
19X1	1X1	3X3	11X1	4X4	19X1	11X2
13X2	3X6	5X1	2X11	13X1	2X7	8X3

WORDS

1. SLEET
2. RIVERS
3. GRAPES
4. FRUITS

EASY

2X11	12X2	3X3	3X4	7X1	5X5	6X4
4X3	6X2	5X1	2X7	2X3	2X1	19X1
2X9	3X3	2X11	3X3	12X2	2X10	13X2
4X5	2X2	5X5	1X1	3X7	3X8	2X7
19X1	2X9	3X3	4X4	2X9	7X1	2X11
3X1	7X1	3X1	3X5	3X3	5X1	17X1
19X1	3X3	4X5	3X4	2X2	2X9	5X5

WORDS

1. CRYING
2. GRAVEL
3. STUPID
4. IDIOTIC

EASY

3X5	4X5	2X10	2X11	4X6	9X2	19X1
17X1	5X1	2X3	4X5	23X1	3X7	2X11
5X1	12X2	2X4	13X2	2X7	11X2	13X1
11X1	2X7	3X4	3X3	19X1	5X5	4X4
2X9	4X4	3X3	2X4	2X7	11X1	1X1
1X1	3X5	3X6	1X1	1X1	4X4	13X1
3X3	7X1	2X10	19X1	2X7	2X2	13X2

WORDS

1. SUNSHINE
2. PASTOR
3. THINK
4. GRANDMA

EASY

23X1	1X1	2X2	5X3	2X9	5X4	2X8
5X1	2X10	5X5	3X3	7X1	5X1	1X1
12X2	2X7	2X4	7X1	13X1	11X2	4X5
11X1	5X1	13X2	3X3	3X2	3X6	4X5
2X1	8X3	4X3	7X1	2X9	2X10	5X1
4X6	17X1	3X3	3X1	2X9	3X3	3X1
19X1	2X7	5X1	6X3	3X5	2X7	2X11

WORDS

1. BENEATH
2. TRIGGER
3. CONCERT
4. VIRGIN

EASY

1X1	13X1	7X1	3X4	8X3	5X5	4X3
5X2	2X8	2X10	2X9	2X11	13X2	12X2
5X1	3X5	4X4	2X1	3X5	4X5	4X3
3X5	2X11	1X1	3X3	2X9	2X11	2X1
3X2	5X1	3X4	3X5	5X1	2X2	1X1
23X1	2X11	2X7	2X6	4X4	11X2	11X1
19X1	17X1	4X5	19X1	3X2	19X1	4X4

WORDS

1. APPROVE
2. FOOTBALL
3. SPORT
4. EVENTS

EASY

5X5	2X1	23X1	3X7	3X6	8X3	8X4
4X4	3X4	12X2	5X1	13X1	19X1	2X8
4X3	2X2	1X1	19X1	5X2	19X1	2X11
2X10	4X5	19X1	3X1	4X4	1X1	5X1
3X2	3X3	11X1	5X1	19X1	2X10	19X1
23X1	3X7	8X2	9X2	3X6	5X1	1X1
11X1	13X2	23X1	2X11	2X2	4X5	7X1

WORDS

1. DRESSER
2. VASES
3. GATES
4. BLACK

EASY

4X4	5X4	5X1	2X4	19X1	23X1	2X1
2X11	19X1	3X2	3X3	3X4	3X7	4X5
3X3	4X3	12X2	5X1	19X1	3X2	13X2
13X1	19X1	17X1	19X1	2X4	3X3	5X1
2X2	17X1	19X1	5X1	19X1	3X2	3X7
23X1	2X10	3X7	5X1	19X1	2X4	2X3
3X4	5X5	2X10	3X3	2X8	9X2	2X11

WORDS

1. SELFISH
2. QUITE
3. FISHES
4. BUSHES

EASY

2X1	3X3	3X1	2X4	2X10	3X2	5X1
19X1	4X5	2X1	5X1	1X1	17X1	4X4
5X5	3X7	1X1	19X1	11X1	3X2	3X3
11X2	4X4	3X3	3X3	13X2	23X1	11X1
12X2	7X1	3X4	2X7	3X3	5X5	4X6
3X8	2X2	2X7	3X3	7X1	2X6	2X8
9X2	3X3	3X7	2X7	2X6	5X3	5X1

WORDS

1. BUILD
2. WILLING
3. FAKING
4. PATCHES

EASY

12X2	3X4	7X1	2X7	1X1	23X1	5X5
5X3	13X1	5X1	2X6	3X3	7X1	4X4
2X11	3X3	2X10	7X1	2X10	3X5	3X4
3X4	2X7	5X1	2X7	3X4	19X1	2X4
5X4	5X1	1X1	2X2	23X1	3X5	2X10
4X5	1X1	17X1	3X3	2X9	4X5	19X1
7X1	3X4	7X1	5X1	4X4	13X1	13X2

WORDS

1. GOLDEN
2. TRIANGLE
3. HOSTING
4. MILEAGE

EASY

4X5	2X8	4X4	2X11	2X10	3X2	19X1
3X3	3X4	17X1	19X1	3X2	13X1	3X3
13X2	5X1	5X1	3X4	5X1	2X7	23X1
4X5	3X3	1X1	2X8	7X1	2X9	2X2
3X8	4X4	2X1	19X1	3X7	4X3	12X2
3X6	7X1	5X5	2X7	19X1	2X7	19X1
3X7	3X5	23X1	4X4	1X1	19X1	8X2

WORDS

1. GOWNS
2. SINGLE
3. BYPASS
4. PLEASURE

EASY

2X11	5X5	5X1	5X3	3X3	4X4	19X1
17X1	2X10	2X8	13X1	3X7	2X4	3X1
2X9	19X1	7X2	13X2	11X1	5X1	11X2
13X1	5X1	5X5	2X10	1X1	4X4	5X5
5X1	2X1	19X1	3X2	3X3	2X10	4X1
3X4	4X4	13X1	5X1	19X1	5X1	17X1
7X1	5X1	4X6	3X7	2X7	23X1	3X6

WORDS

1. CHEATER
2. SYSTEM
3. EXPEL
4. NUMBER

EASY

5X3	4X5	2X7	4X4	2X11	5X5	2X10
5X1	5X1	3X4	5X5	3X5	3X7	2X8
19X1	3X6	2X2	3X3	2X6	19X1	23X1
1X1	1X1	5X1	3X7	2X10	4X4	2X11
5X1	11X2	3X6	13X2	11X1	13X1	17X1
5X5	3X1	4X4	5X3	2X8	5X1	3X8
5X1	17X1	2X7	3X3	2X3	3X1	12X2

WORDS

1. STUDENT
2. YEARLY
3. INCREASE
4. EMPLOY

EASY

7X1	2X3	4X3	4X4	5X3	6X3	3X7
1X1	5X5	23X1	5X5	12X2	13X1	19X1
17X1	2X9	2X9	23X1	2X4	2X11	2X4
3X7	2X7	3X4	19X1	11X2	3X1	2X5
13X2	11X1	3X3	5X1	23X1	5X1	2X10
2X5	3X3	2X2	4X3	2X7	7X1	3X5
4X4	2X7	3X2	3X3	2X10	2X7	2X11

WORDS

1. GARNISH
2. JEWELRY
3. NOTCH
4. FINDING

EASY

3X3	12X2	13X1	3X4	19X1	17X1	2X8
3X7	2X7	3X5	5X5	19X1	5X3	3X3
3X5	3X5	2X4	3X1	3X4	2X6	5X4
13X1	2X2	3X1	2X5	5X1	1X1	2X8
13X1	3X5	3X2	5X1	4X5	2X10	3X1
12X2	23X1	3X1	2X11	11X2	3X3	2X7
11X1	13X2	23X1	2X4	2X7	1X1	13X1

WORDS

1. COMMON
2. TECHNICAL
3. SCHOOLS
4. MANTEL

EASY

2X2	3X4	2X4	12X2	13X1	19X1	1X1
11X2	2X10	3X6	1X1	5X1	13X1	13X2
3X6	2X2	2X9	7X1	5X1	2X7	3X7
5X5	4X3	3X3	19X1	1X1	2X1	2X10
2X11	3X1	4X5	2X1	2X9	5X1	4X3
5X4	4X2	5X1	3X5	2X1	5X1	2X2
17X1	19X1	4X5	3X2	3X2	19X1	23X1

WORDS

1. BIRTH
2. EFFECTS
3. BEARD
4. STORAGE

EASY

3X3	2X11	2X10	2X8	2X9	2X7	4X4
5X3	2X7	5X5	2X11	3X5	13X1	11X2
12X2	2X7	2X4	3X4	3X3	13X2	3X6
19X1	3X1	3X5	19X1	1X1	7X1	3X5
17X1	3X3	19X1	2X11	2X7	3X2	5X1
2X9	5X1	1X1	5X4	2X7	2X2	3X3
2X11	19X1	2X10	5X1	3X3	2X1	23X1

WORDS

1. RICHLAND
2. INNOVATE
3. SESSION
4. INFORM

EASY

2X11	3X3	4X3	5X5	13X2	1X1	11X2
4X3	2X3	3X4	12X2	13X2	19X1	17X1
5X1	5X3	3X1	1X1	5X2	2X7	2X9
13X2	3X1	2X9	5X1	2X7	3X3	5X1
2X11	23X1	5X5	2X7	5X1	9X2	23X1
2X8	3X8	2X10	4X5	3X2	3X4	3X5
2X10	3X1	2X11	2X9	1X1	3X4	2X10

WORDS

1. CENTRAL
2. NINETY
3. CRAZY
4. FLOWERS

EASY

2X1	19X1	2X9	17X1	3X3	5X1	4X4
5X5	2X11	3X7	5X1	2X8	2X1	2X2
13X2	1X1	3X3	4X4	4X5	13X1	11X2
23X1	2X6	3X4	5X1	19X1	3X6	2X5
6X3	3X2	19X1	2X7	1X1	3X5	4X4
4X3	12X2	2X10	4X4	13X1	13X2	23X1
2X11	3X3	2X7	5X1	10X2	19X1	17X1

WORDS

1. RAMPS
2. VALENTINE
3. POSTER
4. FLIPPED

EASY

2X1	13X2	2X11	19X1	2X3	3X3	5X1
5X3	5X1	4X3	12X2	13X2	3X4	2X2
2X9	2X11	2X10	4X4	23X1	7X1	9X2
2X8	3X1	4X5	3X2	3X5	1X1	3X7
3X5	3X3	1X1	5X1	3X2	3X5	11X2
3X6	3X5	12X2	2X6	5X1	13X2	7X1
11X2	2X4	11X1	3X3	5X5	19X1	7X3

WORDS

1. LETTER
2. AFFAIR
3. GOOGLE
4. COOKIES

EASY

2X2	23X1	4X5	3X6	5X5	2X6	7X1
17X1	2X8	19X1	5X1	1X1	3X8	3X2
3X7	4X5	6X2	2X7	5X1	13X1	3X5
2X11	1X1	7X3	2X10	4X5	6X4	2X9
3X3	3X3	5X1	1X1	3X1	5X1	12X2
19X1	2X1	2X9	3X4	5X1	2X2	17X1
2X3	4X3	12X2	13X2	19X1	2X10	2X11

WORDS

1. VIBRATE
2. CLEATS
3. RENTED
4. GLAMOR

EASY

2X9	5X1	3X3	4X1	12X2	13X2	13X1
7X1	5X1	2X11	4X4	4X5	19X1	5X5
2X8	1X1	5X2	3X5	13X2	4X5	17X1
4X4	7X1	5X1	7X1	1X1	3X3	4X1
2X7	3X5	3X1	13X1	2X1	23X1	2X11
5X1	2X4	19X1	2X6	11X2	13X1	11X1
13X2	4X4	3X4	5X5	5X1	3X7	2X9

WORDS

1. ENGAGE
2. STABLE
3. CHOPPER
4. POEMS

EASY

2X1	3X4	5X5	19X1	23X1	1X1	2X11
1X1	3X2	5X1	5X1	3X4	11X2	4X5
2X9	23X1	2X9	3X3	3X3	5X1	1X1
5X1	1X1	23X1	2X2	13X2	2X8	17X1
2X2	19X1	3X5	12X2	13X1	4X5	5X5
2X7	2X1	3X3	2X9	3X7	19X1	12X2
3X7	5X1	3X6	2X9	2X8	2X1	4X3

WORDS

1. AWARE
2. BODIES
3. SURRENDER
4. PILATE

EASY

3X3	12X2	13X1	19X1	2X7	17X1	3X2
3X1	2X4	19X1	3X3	3X5	7X1	5X1
4X4	3X4	5X1	2X7	13X1	2X9	12X2
13X2	13X1	3X1	3X5	3X1	1X1	9X2
3X7	3X6	3X3	11X1	3X3	7X1	8X2
2X2	4X5	5X1	3X1	5X4	13X1	2X11
2X10	1X1	2X10	19X1	4X5	6X3	4X6

WORDS

1. CHECKER
2. GAMING
3. STATIONS
4. MICRO

EASY

2X11	13X2	1X1	11X2	19X1	3X1	11X1
13X2	19X1	17X1	2X10	3X3	2X6	4X2
4X4	2X7	19X1	3X3	2X1	5X1	19X1
23X1	1X1	2X9	1X1	5X1	5X1	2X4
5X4	3X4	3X6	3X7	2X9	2X4	2X8
3X2	2X10	4X4	2X1	2X2	3X4	4X4
5X5	23X1	3X7	3X5	6X4	4X4	12X2

WORDS

1. PLASTIC
2. HEART
3. BURN
4. HEELS

EASY

2X11	13X2	2X6	19X1	3X4	5X5	5X3
5X4	1X1	3X7	8X2	2X2	7X1	12X2
19X1	12X2	3X7	3X4	2X1	3X4	5X3
2X9	3X8	2X11	5X1	3X5	3X6	23X1
5X1	3X5	13X1	13X2	19X1	5X1	17X1
3X4	19X1	3X6	2X2	5X1	19X1	1X1
11X2	2X3	2X10	1X1	4X3	5X5	2X1

WORDS

1. GLOSSY
2. SEXUAL
3. ARMOR
4. BREEZE

EASY

7X1	19X1	2X8	2X3	3X3	5X1	3X7
12X2	1X1	13X2	17X1	19X1	19X1	7X1
13X1	5X1	2X2	4X5	3X6	5X5	3X3
4X4	2X9	2X2	23X1	5X1	3X5	23X1
3X7	3X5	2X9	3X4	8X3	2X4	3X2
11X1	3X2	5X1	2X11	2X1	2X2	2X10
1X1	3X1	3X3	2X7	3X7	1X1	11X2

WORDS

1. WRECK
2. SADDLE
3. HORSES
4. UNIFORM

EASY

4X5	5X5	3X2	5X3	3X3	19X1	2X11
17X1	2X8	4X4	3X7	23X1	2X10	5X1
3X4	3X8	5X1	3X3	3X6	3X1	12X2
13X2	19X1	13X1	2X2	11X2	11X1	3X1
19X1	5X5	2X9	1X1	4X3	1X1	4X4
3X3	3X6	3X4	5X1	13X1	2X1	12X2
13X1	19X1	5X1	4X4	11X1	3X3	17X1

WORDS

1. PEDAL
2. BIKERS
3. CRUISE
4. PAMPERS

EASY

5X3	5X1	2X11	2X10	4X5	12X2	19X1
2X10	23X1	3X5	17X1	3X2	3X8	2X1
3X3	5X1	2X2	2X9	12X2	13X2	2X8
19X1	2X1	3X2	7X1	4X3	3X3	4X4
5X5	5X3	1X1	5X1	3X1	13X2	17X1
3X4	19X1	2X9	2X7	11X1	19X1	2X5
3X7	1X1	2X9	3X3	2X8	3X8	2X1

WORDS

1. ORGAN
2. SPIRAL
3. WEBSITE
4. PICKER

EASY

2X11	4X4	19X1	7X1	3X3	5X1	13X1
12X2	1X1	11X1	3X1	2X7	11X2	2X7
17X1	2X9	3X1	3X3	19X1	3X6	3X1
3X3	2X4	2X10	2X6	5X1	5X1	5X5
5X4	1X1	4X4	3X4	3X1	2X10	12X2
13X2	17X1	2X9	1X1	5X1	19X1	3X2
5X4	13X2	4X3	2X8	3X7	3X1	23X1

WORDS

1. CHARACTER
2. PARTING
3. CELLS
4. SCIENCE

EASY

2X11	19X1	13X2	4X4	3X6	7X2	2X8
5X1	19X1	2X1	2X1	5X1	3X7	9X2
2X11	3X4	3X1	2X10	2X1	2X8	3X3
12X2	13X1	5X1	19X1	2X2	17X1	1X1
11X1	2X7	4X4	19X1	11X2	5X1	2X2
3X3	2X4	5X1	19X1	2X6	3X1	1X1
2X10	19X1	17X1	3X3	2X9	2X1	7X1

WORDS

1. SCENES
2. CRISP
3. PEBBLES
4. ABLED

EASY

2X11	3X3	2X2	5X1	2X9	2X2	3X4
4X4	5X1	5X3	3X7	3X1	6X4	5X1
3X7	3X1	2X1	4X5	3X5	11X2	3X1
11X1	19X1	1X1	3X2	2X7	1X1	17X1
4X3	5X3	2X10	3X7	3X5	2X7	5X5
6X3	6X2	3X6	13X1	2X9	12X2	19X1
17X1	1X1	23X1	12X2	5X5	13X2	13X1

WORDS

1. FURNACE
2. STRAW
3. ECONOMY
4. DECATUR

EASY

19X1	2X10	2X9	3X1	2X10	2X1	4X5
2X11	5X1	3X3	1X1	3X4	5X1	23X1
3X3	2X9	13X1	4X3	4X5	3X2	8X2
3X8	12X2	2X10	19X1	3X3	1X1	13X1
13X2	12X2	3X3	2X11	2X6	2X2	9X2
4X5	3X4	7X1	5X5	3X5	6X3	7X3
12X2	5X1	2X6	1X1	11X2	19X1	3X3

WORDS

1. VILLAGE
2. FLAMER
3. DISTRICT
4. ISOLATE

ANSWERS

		19X1=S (2)				
	3X6=R (2)				4X5=T (3)	
	5X1=E (2)	19X1=S (1)		2X7=N (3)		
	7X1=G (1)	2X6=L (2)		3X3=I (3)	19X1=S (1)	
	3X4=L (2)	2X7=N (1)		1X1=A (1)	3X5=O (3)	8X2=P (3)
	2X7=N (4)	5X1=E (2)	3X3=I (1)	2X11=V (1)		
19X1=S (4)	2X10=T (2)	5X1=E (4)	2X11=V (4)	3X5=O (4)		

					2X7=N (3)	
2X7=N (1)		7X1=G (1)			5X1=E (3)	
	1X1=A (1)	19X1=S (2)	5X1=E (1)	2X9=R (3)		
5X5=Y (4)		11X1=K (2)	2X11=V (1)	5X1=E (2)	2X2=D (3)	
	1X1=A (4)	3X5=O (4)	5X1=E (2)		7X1=G (2)	19X1=S (3)
	2X2=D (4)		2X10=T (4)			

			2X7=N (3)	7X1=G (3)		
		3X1=C (3)	11X1=K (2)	3X3=I (3)		
	1X1=A (3)	2X7=N (2)	2X10=T (3)			
		3X5=O (2)				3X6=R (4)
			23X1=W (2)	3X4=L (4)	19X1=S (1)	5X1=E (4)
		4X5=T (1)	3X3=I (2)	1X1=A (4)	2X4=H (1)	2X11=V (4)
	7X1=G (2)	2X7=N (2)	3X6=R (1)	3X3=I (1)	5X1=E (4)	

				3X6=R (3)		
			5X1=E (3)			
	19X1=S (2)		2X6=L (3)	19X1=S (1)	8X3=X (3)	19X1=S (4)
		2X8=P (2)		1X1=A (3)	5X1=E (1)	11X1=K (4)
		3X3=I (2)	2X4=H (1)		13X1=M (1)	3X5=O (4)
	3X1=C (2)			3X5=O (1)	3X5=O (4)	
		5X1=E (2)				2X6=L (4)

2X7=N (1)					19X1=S (4)
1X1=A (1)				2X4=H (4)	
	13X1=M (1)			11X1=K (4)	3X5=O (4)
5X5=Y (2)	3X5=O (1)	2X7=N (2)	5X1=E (2)	5X1=E (3)	3X1=C (4)
	3X4=L (2)	23X1=W (1)	2X11=V (3)	2X11=V (2)	
2X1=B (3)	5X1=E (3)		5X1=E (3)	5X1=E (2)	
		2X6=L (3)	3X3=I (3)		

	3X4=L (1)				
		3X5=O (1)			19X1=S (4)
	2X11=V (1)		4X4=P (2)	19X1=S (4)	
	5X1=E (1)	5X1=E (2)	1X1=A (2)	5X1=E (4)	
2X2=D (1)	2X9=R (2)	1X1=A (3)		2X8=P (2)	3X6=R (4)
2X1=B (3)	5X5=Y (3)		13X1=M (3)		2X2=D (4)
5X1=E (3)					

			5X1=E (4)	3X6=R (4)			
		2X4=H (4)					
	2X10=T (4)	7X1=G (2)	2X9=R (2)	5X1=E (1)			
	3X5=O (4)		3X4=L (1)	1X1=A (2)			
		13X1=M (4)	4X4=P (1)	5X4=T (2)	2X7=N (2)		
				1X1=A (1)	2X7=N (1)	19X1=S (3)	
		2X9=R (3)	3X7=U (3)	3X3=I (3)	2X7=N (3)	19X1=S (1)	

			2X9=R (1)			
		3X5=O (1)		4X5=T (2)		
	2X10=T (3)	19X1=S (1)	3X1=C (2)			2X7=N (4)
	2X4=H (3)	5X1=E (2)	2X7=N (1)		5X1=E (4)	
7X1=G (3)	19X1=S (1)	2X7=N (2)	3X5=O (1)			2X11=V (4)
	3X3=I (3)	4X4=P (1)	2X7=N (2)	3X5=O (2)	3X1=C (2)	3X3=I (4)
	2X9=R (3)				7X1=G (4)	

			3X1=C (2)	5X1=E (2)		
		3X3=I (2)	5X1=E (1)	3X1=C (1)		3X5=O (3)
		3X3=I (1)	2X11=V (2)	5X1=E (1)	2X9=R (3)	19X1=S (3)
	2X7=N (1)		2X9=R (2)		2X6=L (3)	5X1=E (3)
	7X1=G (4)	2X7=N (4)	5X1=E (2)	5X1=E (3)		
19X1=S (4)		19X1=S (2)	3X3=I (4)		13X1=M (3)	
				11X1=K (4)		

	2X7=N (1)		5X1=E (2)			
5X1=E (1)		2X10=T (1)		3X1=C (2)	2X10=T (4)	
2X2=D (1)	3X4=L (3)	3X3=I (1)		3X7=U (4)	3X3=I (2)	5X1=E (4)
	19X1=S (1)	5X1=E (3)	2X7=N (4)		3X2=F (2)	
	2X5=J (3)	4X5=T (1)	3X3=I (4)	3X2=F (2)		
		1X1=A (3)	2X9=R (3)	13X1=M (4)	3X5=O (2)	
			3X5=O (3)			

		2X9=R (2)				
	5X1=E (2)					13X1=M (3)
	7X1=G (2)	5X1=E (1)			3X5=O (3)	
5X5=Y (4)	3X3=I (1)	3X6=R (2)			2X2=D (3)	
3X2=F (4)	1X1=A (2)	2X10=T (1)	2X7=N (1)	1X1=A (1)		5X1=E (3)
3X3=I (4)	2X4=H (2)	1X1=A (4)		3X7=U (1)	3X4=L (3)	
3X1=C (2)	2X6=L (4)		3X7=U (4)	17X1=Q (4)		

	3X2=F (4)			2X7=N (2)		
		2X9=R (4)	2X2=D (4)	1X1=A (2)	5X5=Y (4)	
		3X3=I (4)	2X11=V (2)	1X1=A (4)		
		5X1=E (1)	5X1=E (3)	1X1=A (2)		
		7X1=G (1)	2X9=R (2)	2X7=N (3)	3X3=I (3)	
	3X1=C (2)	1X1=A (2)	2X2=D (1)	3X5=O (1)	2X6=L (3)	
			3X5=O (3)	2X7=N (3)	2X2=D (1)	

				19X1=S (1)	4X5=T (1)	
		3X6=R (1)		1X1=A (1)		
	2X2=D (1)	1X1=A (1)	13X1=M (3)	2X7=N (1)		2X2=D (4)
		19X1=S (3)	2X2=D (1)	1X1=A (3)	5X1=E (3)	5X1=E (4)
	3X4=L (2)	2X2=D (2)	5X1=E (2)	3X3=I (4)	2X7=N (4)	2X10=T (3)
	3X3=I (2)	1X1=A (2)		13X1=M (2)	3X5=O (4)	
		3X1=C (2)			2X5=J (4)	

			2X4=H (2)			
		10X2=T (4)	4X5=T (2)	19X1=S (1)		
	3X3=I (4)	2X7=N (3)	3X7=U (1)	23X1=W (2)	4X5=T (1)	
	3X6=R (3)	13X1=M (4)	2X2=D (1)	2X9=R (1)	3X5=O (2)	
1X1=A (3)	3X3=I (1)	2X7=N (1)	13X1=M (4)	3X6=R (2)	5X5=Y (1)	
	5X1=E (3)	3X4=L (3)	3X5=O (4)	7X1=G (2)		
			3X1=C (4)			

		19X1=S (2)		19X1=S (4)	
	5X1=E (3)	23X1=W (2)		3X3=I (4)	
	3X3=I (2)	2X7=N (3)	3X5=O (3)	2X8=P (3)	3X4=L (4)
2X9=R (1)	3X6=R (2)	2X6=L (2)	2X11=V (1)	2X4=H (3)	2X11=V (4)
5X1=E (1)		3X3=I (1)		5X1=E (4)	
	23X1=W (1)	5X1=E (1)	2X9=R (4)		

			6X2=L (3)	2X2=D (2)	5X1=E (4)
			1X1=A (3)		3X3=I (2)
		19X1=S (3)			1X1=A (2)
2X7=N (1)	2X10=T (3)			3X4=L (4)	13X1=M (2)
3X3=I (3)	3X5=O (1)	2X2=D (2)	2X1=B (1)	3X5=O (2)	4X4=P (4)
2X7=N (3)	4X5=T (1)	3X7=U (1)	2X7=N (2)	6X4=X (4)	
	7X1=G (3)	2X10=T (1)			5X1=E (4)

		3X5=O (2)		2X9=R (4)	3X5=O (4)	
2X7=N (2)			19X1=S (2)		4X4=P (2)	3X4=L (4)
		3X7=U (3)	3X3=I (3)	3X6=R (2)	5X1=E (2)	3X3=I (4)
	19X1=S (3)		2X8=P (1)	4X5=T (3)	1X1=A (4)	
		5X1=E (1)	5X1=E (3)	2X4=H (1)		2X10=T (4)
		1X1=A (1)	3X1=C (1)			

						3X1=C (4)
	5X1=E (3)			3X1=C (2)	2X4=H (4)	
	5X5=Y (3)	2X1=B (3)	2X9=R (3)	3X5=O (2)	5X1=E (4)	
	5X1=E (3)	5X1=E (1)	13X1=M (2)	3X5=O (3)		5X1=E (4)
		3X3=I (2)	2X6=L (1)	23X1=W (3)	19X1=S (1)	11X1=K (4)
		2X7=N (2)	3X3=I (1)	13X1=M (1)		19X1=S (4)
			7X1=G (2)			

19X1=S (1)						
	3X7=U (1)			2X8=P (3)		
	3X6=R (1)			3X4=L (3)	2X10=T (4)	3X1=C (2)
	19X1=S (3)	4X4=P (1)	3X7=U (3)	3X5=O (4)	3X5=O (2)	
		13X1=M (3)	2X9=R (1)	3X5=O (4)	13X1=M (2)	
			3X3=I (1)	3X2=F (2)	2X4=H (4)	4X5=T (2)
		19X1=S (1)	5X1=E (1)	3X5=O (2)	2X9=R (2)	19X1=S (4)

		1X1=A (3)				
			2X2=D (3)		13X1=M (2)	
		13X1=M (3)		1X1=A (2)		
		2X9=R (3)	3X3=I (3)	3X3=I (2)		
	5X1=E (3)	3X5=O (1)	4X5=T (1)	2X7=N (2)	19X1=S (1)	11X1=K (4)
	2X7=N (1)			5X1=E (1)	5X1=E (2)	3X1=C (4)
			3X1=C (4)	2X6=L (4)	3X3=I (4)	

	19X1=S (2)		2X7=N (2)			7X1=G (4)
		11X1=K (2)		1X1=A (2)	2X7=N (4)	
		23X1=W (3)	1X1=A (3)	2X4=H (2)	3X3=I (4)	
		19X1=S (1)		3X4=L (3)	2X10=T (2)	11X1=K (4)
5X1=E (1)	2X1=B (1)			2X7=N (3)	3X5=O (4)	
		19X1=S (1)	3X5=O (1)	3X5=O (4)	3X3=I (3)	
		19X1=S (1)		2X4=H (4)		

			23X1=W (4)	1X1=A (4)		
3X6=R (4)	3X1=C (2)	5X5=Y (4)			2X6=L (4)	
		5X1=E (4)	2X4=H (2)	13X1=M (1)		
			3X7=U (2)	3X5=O (1)	11X1=K (2)	4X5=T (3)
		11X1=K (1)	2X7=N (1)	2X7=N (2)	5X1=E (3)	
		5X1=E (1)	23X1=W (3)	5X1=E (3)		
		19X1=S (3)	5X5=Y (1)			

		2X2=D (4)	5X1=E (4)			
	2X7=N (2)			5X1=E (4)		
7X1=G (2)		3X3=I (2)		3X1=C (4)		
	19X1=S (1)	3X4=L (2)	2X2=D (1)		3X1=C (4)	2X8=P (3)
		5X1=E (1)	2X6=L (2)	3X5=O (1)	3X7=U (4)	2X9=R (3)
		19X1=S (3)	3X3=I (2)	19X1=S (4)	3X1=C (1)	3X5=O (3)
		2X1=B (2)	19X1=S (3)	5X1=E (3)	3X1=C (3)	

		5X1=E (1)				
		5X1=E (2)	2X9=R (1)	3X7=U (1)		
	3X6=R (2)	5X1=E (2)	19X1=S (1)			4X5=T (4)
		2X7=N (1)	3X6=R (2)		2X9=R (4)	
			3X3=I (1)	1X1=A (2)	11X1=K (3)	5X1=E (4)
		2X9=R (3)	3X5=O (3)	3X5=O (3)	3X1=C (2)	3X4=L (4)
		2X1=B (3)			1X1=A (4)	

PAGE 31

			5X1=E (3)	2X4=H (3)		
		2X2=D (3)		7X1=G (2)	3X1=C (3)	
	3X2=F (4)	2X9=R (3)	2X7=N (2)	1X1=A (3)		
		3X5=O (4)	5X1=E (3)	3X3=I (2)	19X1=S (1)	
2X7=N (4)	3X7=U (4)	11X1=K (1)	3X3=I (1)	2X11=V (2)	2X6=L (1)	
5X1=E (4)	19X1=S (1)	2X9=R (4)	3X5=O (2)	3X4=L (1)		
	5X1=E (4)	2X10=T (4)		13X1=M (2)		

PAGE 32

		4X5=T (2)				
			3X6=R (2)	3X7=U (2)		
	2X7=N (3)	7X1=G (3)	5X1=E (4)	3X1=C (4)	3X1=C (2)	
3X7=U (3)	2X7=N (3)	3X2=F (4)	2X2=D (1)	11X1=K (2)	2X10=T (4)	
2X9=R (3)		3X3=I (3)	5X1=E (4)	5X1=E (1)	2X4=H (1)	
	19X1=S (3)	2X2=D (4)	1X1=A (1)	4X5=T (1)		

			7X1=G (3)	2X7=N (2)			
		3X6=R (1)	3X3=I (2)	2X7=N (3)	7X1=G (2)		
3X4=L (4)	1X1=A (2)	19X1=S (2)	3X5=O (1)		3X5=O (3)		
5X1=E (2)	1X1=A (4)	2X9=R (4)	13X1=M (1)	3X6=R (3)	2X4=H (1)		
	3X4=L (2)	3X5=O (4)	2X10=T (3)	3X7=U (1)			
			3X1=C (4)	19X1=S (3)			

			19X1=S (1)	19X1=S (4)	3X1=C (2)	3X3=I (4)
		3X2=F (1)	4X5=T (4)	3X3=I (2)	2X7=N (4)	5X1=E (2)
	2X6=L (4)	5X1=E (1)	1X1=A (4)	2X10=T (2)		
		3X4=L (4)	5X1=E (1)	19X1=S (2)		
	4X4=P (3)	2X9=R (3)	3X7=U (2)	3X6=R (1)	19X1=S (3)	
		2X5=J (2)	3X5=O (3)	2X8=P (3)		

		19X1=S (2)				
		5X1=E (1)	11X1=K (2)	5X1=E (4)		
3X8=X (1)	3X6=R (2)	19X1=S (1)			3X4=L (4)	
	3X5=O (1)	1X1=A (2)	7X1=G (4)		23X1=W (3)	
23X1=W (4)	2X1=B (1)	7X1=G (4)	4X4=P (2)	1X1=A (3)		
	3X3=I (4)	19X1=S (3)	19X1=S (2)	3X4=L (3)		
			2X6=L (3)			

2X8=P (1)				7X1=G (4)		
	3X5=O (1)		2X7=N (4)	4X5=T (3)	5X1=E (4)	
	19X1=S (1)	1X1=A (4)		2X9=R (3)		
	2X4=H (4)	19X1=S (1)			1X1=A (3)	
	3X1=C (4)	3X3=I (1)	2X7=N (2)	2X6=L (1)	13X1=M (3)	1X1=A (3)
		3X5=O (2)	2X1=B (1)	2X2=D (2)	5X1=E (1)	3X1=C (2)
	3X1=C (2)				3X7=U (2)	2X10=T (2)

			5X5=Y (4)	2X9=R (1)	3X7=U (4)	
			5X1=E (1)	4X5=T (4)	3X3=I (1)	1X1=A (4)
				13X1=M (1)	2X7=N (1)	5X1=E (4)
				2X2=D (1)	2X1=B (4)	1X1=A (3)
			4X6=X (2)	2X10=T (2)	3X1=C (3)	2X2=D (2)
		5X1=E (2)	13X1=M (3)	5X1=E (3)	5X1=E (2)	3X3=I (3)
		4X5=T (2)		1X1=A (3)	3X6=R (3)	

PAGE 38

	7X1=G (4)			5X1=E (3)		
		2X7=N (4)		19X1=S (3)		2X1=B (4)
		3X3=I (4)	3X6=R (3)	1X1=A (4)	5X1=E (4)	
		13X1=M (2)	2X10=T (4)	5X1=E (3)	5X1=E (1)	
			5X1=E (2)	4X4=P (1)	2X11=V (3)	3X7=U (1)
	1X1=A (2)		2X2=D (2)	3X7=U (1)	3X3=I (3)	19X1=S (1)
		3X3=I (2)	3X7=U (3)	2X7=N (3)	2X9=R (1)	

		5X1=E (1)	19X1=S (1)			2X2=D (4)
		2X7=N (1)	19X1=S (3)		3X3=I (4)	
	19X1=S (3)	5X1=E (3)	5X1=E (1)	5X1=E (2)	19X1=S (4)	
	3X7=U (3)		4X4=P (1)	3X4=L (2)	5X1=E (1)	5X1=E (4)
		1X1=A (3)	3X3=I (2)	3X8=X (1)	2X8=P (2)	1X1=A (4)
		19X1=S (2)	3X1=C (3)	13X1=M (2)	19X1=S (4)	5X1=E (4)

		3X2=F (2)		2X2=D (4)		
	3X3=I (4)	3X4=L (2)	5X1=E (4)			
	7X1=G (4)	19X1=S (4)	3X5=O (2)		5X1=E (1)	
2X7=N (4)		5X1=E (1)	23X1=W (2)	1X1=A (1)	3X2=F (1)	
		2X9=R (1)	3X3=I (2)	2X10=T (1)	7X1=G (2)	19X1=S (3)
			3X7=U (1)	2X7=N (2)	5X1=E (3)	
		19X1=S (3)	1X1=A (3)	3X4=L (3)		

	13X1=M (3)					
		3X5=O (3)				
		2X10=T (3)	3X6=R (2)			2X10=T (4)
		2X4=H (3)	5X1=E (3)	5X1=E (2)	3X7=U (4)	
	5X1=E (2)	1X1=A (1)	2X11=V (2)	2X9=R (3)	2X8=P (1)	2X1=B (4)
	7X1=G (2)	13X2=Z (1)	5X1=E (2)	3X4=L (1)	3X3=I (4)	
		2X7=N (2)	1X1=A (1)	7X1=G (4)	2X7=N (4)	

				3X2=F (4)			
			5X1=E (4)		19X1=S (3)		
		7X1=G (2)	2X2=D (4)	5X1=E (4)	5X1=E (1)	5X1=E (3)	
		3X3=I (4)	3X6=R (2)	13X1=M (1)	2X9=R (3)	19X1=S (1)	
	2X7=N (4)	7X1=G (4)	5X1=E (1)	1X1=A (2)	3X5=O (3)		
	3X1=C (2)	3X3=I (2)	2X4=H (1)	4X4=P (2)		3X1=C (3)	
			2X4=H (2)	4X5=T (1)	19X1=S (3)		

			2X7=N (4)	7X1=G (2)		
			2X9=R (2)	3X3=I (4)	3X7=U (2)	
		1X1=A (2)	1X1=A (4)	5X1=E (2)	5X1=E (3)	
	7X1=G (4)	3X6=R (4)	3X2=F (1)	2X6=L (3)	3X7=U (1)	
				5X1=E (1)	3X5=O (3)	2X2=D (1)
			23X1=W (3)	2X4=H (3)	19X1=S (1)	

		2X9=R (4)		3X4=L (3)		
	3X3=I (4)	2X2=D (1)	3X6=R (4)	2X6=L (3)		
	2X7=N (4)	3X4=L (2)	5X1=E (1)	1X1=A (4)	5X1=E (3)	
7X1=G (4)	5X1=E (2)	13X1=M (1)	7X1=G (2)	5X1=E (4)	3X1=C (1)	2X4=H (3)
			3X6=R (1)	7X1=G (2)	2X4=H (1)	19X1=S (3)
			3X7=U (2)	1X1=A (1)		
			2X5=J (2)			

				2X4=H (3)			
			3X1=C (3)				
	19X1=S (1)	2X9=R (4)	4X5=T (4)	1X1=A (3)	7X1=G (1)		
	3X1=C (4)	2X10=T (1)	5X1=E (4)	2X7=N (1)	3X5=O (3)	3X1=C (3)	
	5X1=E (4)	1X1=A (1)	4X5=T (2)	3X3=I (1)			
	19X1=S (4)	5X1=E (2)	7X1=G (1)	1X1=A (2)			
				2X2=D (2)	4X4=P (2)	3X7=U (2)	

		2X10=T (2)				
	1X1=A (2)		5X1=E (2)			
		2X6=L (2)		2X2=D (1)	2X2=D (4)	3X6=R (1)
		3X5=O (2)	2X7=N (1)	2X9=R (4)	5X1=E (1)	2X7=N (3)
		5X1=E (1)	3X1=C (2)	3X5=O (2)	1X1=A (4)	3X6=R (3)
			7X1=G (1)	2X4=H (2)	3X7=U (3)	5X1=E (4)
		2X9=R (3)	5X1=E (3)	2X10=T (3)	3X1=C (2)	2X4=H (4)

			5X1=E (2)			
3X1=C (1)	19X1=S (1)	2X6=L (2)				12X1=L (4)
2X1=B (1)	3X4=L (1)		2X1=B (2)		5X1=E (4)	
3X7=U (1)			2X1=B (2)		2X11=V (4)	
		3X7=U (2)	3X4=L (3)	3X3=I (3)	5X1=E (4)	3X1=C (3)
		2X6=L (3)	2X1=B (2)	18X1=R (4)	2X4=H (3)	
		5X1=E (4)	7X1=G (4)	1X1=A (4)		

		3X3=I (2)	2X7=N (1)	3X3=I (1)		
	23X1=W (2)	7X1=G (1)	14X1=N (2)	2X4=H (3)	2X6=L (1)	
	3X5=O (2)	2X2=D (4)	19X1=S (3)	7X1=G (2)	3X3=I (1)	
	2X9=R (4)	2X4=H (2)	3X7=U (3)	3X2=F (1)		
	3X5=O (4)	19X1=S (2)	2X7=N (4)	3X4=L (3)		
		23X1=W (4)			2X1=B (3)	

		13X1=M (2)				
			3X5=O (2)			
			19X1=S (2)	19X1=S (4)		
		4X5=T (2)	5X1=E (3)	19X1=S (1)	5X1=E (4)	
	3X4=L (2)	19X1=S (3)	17X1=Q (1)		2X4=H (4)	5X1=E (1)
		5X5=Y (2)	1X1=A (3)	3X7=U (1)	2X9=R (1)	19X1=S (4)
		4X5=T (3)	5X1=E (3)	1X1=A (1)		1X1=A (4)

		2X2=D (2)	3X5=O (3)		19X1=S (3)	3X6=R (4)
		3X4=L (3)	3X6=R (2)	2X9=R (3)	3X3=I (4)	
		3X5=O (3)	3X3=I (2)	3X5=O (4)	19X1=S (1)	
	3X1=C (3)		2X6=L (2)	23X1=W (1)	13X1=M (4)	
		2X10=T (1)	3X4=L (2)	5X1=E (1)	5X1=E (4)	
			1X1=A (1)			13X1=M (4)

				3X5=O (1)			
	3X3=I (3)			5X1=E (3)	3X5=O (1)	19X1=S (4)	
	13X1=M (3)		7X1=G (3)	4X5=T (1)	2X7=N (3)	4X3=L (4)	
		1X1=A (3)	2X10=T (1)	3X3=I (3)	2X7=N (2)	1X1=A (4)	
			1X1=A (1)	3X3=I (2)	5X1=E (4)	7X1=G (2)	
19X1=S (2)	4X4=P (2)	2X9=R (2)	4X5=T (1)			2X2=D (4)	

		2X8=P (4)					
			1X1=A (4)	2X6=L (1)	13X1=M (4)		
			2X2=D (1)	5X5=Y (4)	5X1=E (1)	5X1=E (4)	
	7X1=G (3)		5X1=E (1)	2X9=R (2)	1X1=A (2)	2X7=N (4)	
2X7=N (3)	7X1=G (2)	5X1=E (2)	5X1=E (2)	5X1=E (1)	2X10=T (4)	2X6=L (2)	
	3X3=I (3)	2X2=D (3)	2X7=N (2)	2X7=N (1)			
			1X1=A (3)	5X1=E (3)	3X6=R (3)		

		2X7=N (2)	2X7=N (3)	3X7=U (3)	3X5=O (3)	1X1=A (3)
		3X5=O (2)	2X10=T (3)	3X6=R (1)		13X1=M (3)
23X1=W (4)			4X5=T (2)	5X1=E (1)		
	3X5=O (4)	19X1=S (4)	3X3=I (2)	3X1=C (2)	3X1=C (1)	
	3X6=R (4)	5X1=E (4)	5X1=E (1)	3X3=I (1)	5X1=E (2)	
		3X6=R (4)	3X3=I (4)	2X8=P (1)		

	3X1=C (4)				2X7=N (4)	
		2X4=H (4)	1X1=A (4)	2X7=N (4)		5X1=E (4)
		2X2=D (3)	3X1=C (2)		5X1=E (1)	3X4=L (4)
		5X1=E (3)	1X1=A (2)		3X4=L (1)	5X1=E (3)
		2X8=P (2)	2X11=V (3)	3X3=I (3)	3X1=C (3)	4X5=T (1)
		3X3=I (2)	2X10=T (2)	5X1=E (1)	2X10=T (1)	
			19X1=S (1)	1X1=A (2)	2X6=L (2)	

PAGE 55

				19X1=S (2)		
			3X3=I (4)	2X8=P (4)	2X10=T (2)	
	19X1=S (3)	2X9=R (4)		1X1=A (2)	3X8=X (4)	
	5X1=E (4)	1X1=A (3)	19X1=S (1)	4X5=T (2)	3X4=L (1)	5X1=E (4)
		3X4=L (1)	7X1=G (3)	5X1=E (2)	3X5=O (1)	
		5X1=E (3)	1X1=A (1)	3X1=C (1)	19X1=S (2)	
			2X11=V (3)			

PAGE 56

			3X6=R (4)	5X5=Y (4)		
		5X1=E (4)		4X5=T (3)		
	2X6=L (4)	3X1=C (2)	1X1=A (3)	5X1=E (3)	7X1=G (1)	
	3X4=L (4)	2X1=B (3)	2X9=R (2)	3X4=L (1)	2X2=D (3)	
	1X1=A (4)	5X1=E (3)	3X7=U (2)	3X5=O (1)		
	2X2=D (3)	7X1=G (4)	2X7=N (2)	1X1=A (1)	2X1=B (1)	
			2X6=L (1)	3X1=C (2)	2X4=H (2)	

		3X3=I (1)	2X6=L (3)			
	2X7=N (1)	1X1=A (3)	2X2=D (1)	2X2=D (2)		
	3X1=C (3)	7X1=G (1)	2X7=N (2)	2X6=L (1)	19X1=S (4)	
	3X3=I (3)		3X7=U (2)	5X1=E (1)		2X6=L (4)
		3X2=F (3)	23X1=W (1)	3X5=O (2)	2X1=B (2)	3X4=L (4)
				2X9=R (4)	3X5=O (4)	

			2X9=R (3)	23X1=W (4)		
		5X1=E (3)	3X5=O (4)		5X1=E (4)	
	2X10=T (3)	2X4=H (4)	11X1=K (2)	2X9=R (1)		3X6=R (4)
	19X1=S (4)	19X1=S (3)	2X1=B (1)	3X6=R (2)	3X3=I (1)	
		3X3=I (3)	5X1=E (2)		2X7=N (1)	7X1=G (1)
		2X6=L (2)	7X1=G (3)	5X1=E (3)	3X6=R (3)	
			3X1=C (2)			

		5X1=E (3)		3X3=I (1)	3X3=I (2)	
	1X1=A (3)		2X7=N (1)	1X1=A (2)	1X1=A (1)	7X1=G (2)
	3X6=R (3)			3X4=L (1)	13X1=M (1)	2X9=R (2)
		2X6=L (3)		5X5=Y (1)	3X5=O (2)	
	3X4=L (4)	3X3=I (3)	3X1=C (4)		5X1=E (2)	
3X4=L (4)	5X1=E (3)	1X1=A (4)	5X1=E (4)		7X1=G (2)	
		2X9=R (3)		2X9=R (4)		

	2X7=N (1)	5X1=E (2)				
5X1=E (1)	2X2=D (2)	4X5=T (1)	13X1=M (2)			
2X11=V (1)		3X3=I (1)	13X1=M (2)		1X1=A (3)	2X8=P (4)
			2X7=N (1)	3X3=I (2)	13X1=M (4)	2X7=N (3)
			7X1=G (1)	2X9=R (2)	3X3=I (3)	3X7=U (4)
	1X1=A (3)	2X9=R (3)	3X5=O (3)	3X4=L (3)	2X10=T (2)	3X6=R (4)
		3X1=C (3)			4X5=T (4)	

		19X1=S (1)				
			5X1=E (1)	3X3=I (1)	3X3=I (4)	
		5X1=E (2)	4X4=P (4)	2X8=P (4)	2X2=D (1)	2X7=N (4)
	3X4=L (2)	2X10=T (3)		3X3=I (4)	3X5=O (1)	7X1=G (4)
	11X1=K (2)		3X1=C (3)	3X5=O (1)	2X2=D (4)	
3X6=R (2)		3X3=I (3)	19X1=S (2)	7X1=G (1)		
	1X1=A (2)	4X4=P (2)	2X2=D (3)	2X2=D (3)	1X1=A (3)	

		2X9=R (4)		7X1=G (4)		
	5X1=E (4)		1X1=A (4)	5X1=E (4)		
		2X2=D (4)	2X7=N (1)		2X2=D (1)	
	5X5=Y (3)	3X5=O (1)	7X1=G (1)	2X7=N (2)	3X6=R (1)	5X1=E (2)
		2X9=R (3)	1X1=A (2)	1X1=A (1)	4X5=T (2)	2X2=D (2)
		23X1=W (2)	3X5=O (3)			
			3X4=L (3)	7X1=G (3)		

PAGE 63

			19X1=S (4)		3X5=O (1)	
			2X4=H (4)		3X2=F (1)	
	3X6=R (2)	2X2=D (1)	5X1=E (4)	3X2=F (1)		7X1=G (3)
2X2=D (2)	1X1=A (2)	5X1=E (4)	2X7=N (1)	5X1=E (1)	2X7=N (3)	
		2X10=T (2)	3X6=R (4)		3X3=I (3)	
		19X1=S (2)	3X4=L (3)	13X1=M (2)		4X5=T (3)
		1X1=A (3)	3X7=U (2)	5X1=E (3)	2X9=R (3)	

PAGE 64

				2X2=D (1)		
			3X7=U (4)		5X1=E (1)	
	2X2=D (2)	2X7=N (4)		4X5=T (4)	2X10=T (1)	
19X1=S (2)	3X5=O (4)	3X6=R (2)	1X1=A (2)	2X9=R (1)	19X1=S (4)	
	5X1=E (3)	2X2=D (4)	3X3=I (1)	3X7=U (2)	7X1=G (2)	
		2X6=L (3)	3X4=L (1)	3X5=O (3)	5X1=E (3)	2X8=P (3)
			4X4=P (3)	3X2=F (1)		

	3X4=L (2)	1X1=A (1)		4X4=P (1)	3X3=I (1)	
		1X1=A (2)	19X1=S (1)			2X9=R (1)
	5X1=E (2)	2X2=D (4)			5X1=E (1)	
		13X1=M (2)	5X1=E (4)	5X1=E (4)	3X6=R (4)	3X2=F (4)
		2X10=T (2)	2X2=D (3)	3X5=O (2)		
		5X1=E (3)	1X1=A (2)	2X7=N (3)	3X3=I (3)	2X6=L (3)
			2X9=R (3)			

	2X10=T (4)			3X1=C (1)		
		2X4=H (4)	3X4=L (1)	7X1=G (4)		2X10=T (4)
		3X5=O (4)	3X7=U (4)	3X5=O (1)	2X4=H (4)	
			5X5=Y (2)	19X1=S (1)		
		19X1=S (3)	5X1=E (1)	2X10=T (2)	19X1=S (2)	
		4X5=T (1)	2X10=T (3)	3X7=U (2)	2X2=D (2)	
			2X4=H (3)	7X1=G (3)	3X3=I (3)	4X5=T (3)

			5X1=E (1)	3X6=R (1)	5X5=Y (3)	
		2X4=H (1)		7X1=G (4)	5X1=E (4)	2X2=D (3)
		4X5=T (1)	2X7=N (4)	5X1=E (2)	3X7=U (4)	3X5=O (3)
		3X5=O (4)	5X1=E (1)	19X1=S (2)	2X1=B (3)	
	4X5=T (4)		3X7=U (2)	7X1=G (1)		5X1=E (3)
		3X5=O (2)		3X5=O (1)	13X1=M (3)	
		13X1=M (2)	19X1=S (3)	3X5=O (3)	2X10=T (1)	

		19X1=S (3)				
		3X5=O (3)		23X1=W (1)		
			2X9=R (3)		3X5=O (1)	
		3X4=L (2)	3X6=R (3)	5X5=Y (3)	2X9=R (1)	
		5X1=E (2)	2X4=H (1)	2X10=T (1)	4X5=T (4)	
	1X1=A (2)	7X1=G (2)	2X9=R (4)	5X1=E (4)	2X9=R (4)	
	2X6=L (2)		7X1=G (4)	5X1=E (4)		

13X1=M (1)			19X1=S (4)			
1X1=A (1)	3X4=L (3)	1X1=A (3)		2X10=T (4)	2X8=P (3)	
	19X1=S (1)		2X7=N (3)	5X1=E (3)	3X5=O (4)	
	2X10=T (1)	7X1=G (2)	3X5=O (3)	2X9=R (3)	2X6=L (4)	
	2X7=N (2)	5X1=E (1)		19X1=S (3)	2X9=R (2)	19X1=S (4)
	3X6=R (1)	3X3=I (2)		3X3=I (2)		
			7X1=G (2)	2X7=N (2)		

				2X2=D (1)		
		19X1=S (2)		7X1=G (4)	2X9=R (1)	
	1X1=A (1)	2X7=N (1)	5X1=E (2)	3X5=O (1)	2X7=N (4)	5X1=E (3)
4X5=T (1)		3X3=I (2)	3X2=F (1)	3X3=I (4)	4X5=T (3)	
19X1=S (1)			2X2=D (2)	11X1=K (4)	1X1=A (3)	
	23X1=W (4)	3X5=O (4)	3X6=R (4)	1X1=A (2)	3X4=L (2)	3X1=C (3)
			5X1=E (3)	2X2=D (3)	3X7=U (3)	

2X1=B (1)	3X5=O (3)	19X1=S (3)	3X3=I (3)			
4X4=P (3)	3X7=U (1)	2X10=T (1)	3X3=I (2)	4X5=T (3)		
5X1=E (3)	7X1=G (2)	2X7=N (2)	4X5=T (1)	2X4=H (2)		
	2X2=D (3)	2X7=N (4)	5X1=E (1)	19X1=S (2)		
	2X2=D (4)	3X6=R (1)	3X7=U (4)	3X2=F (4)	3X7=U (2)	
			5X1=E (4)		2X9=R (2)	
			2X9=R (4)			

			2X7=N (2)	2X8=P (1)		
		3X3=I (2)		7X1=G (2)	2X9=R (1)	4X5=T (4)
	2X4=H (2)	2X10=T (1)	3X5=O (1)	2X2=D (3)	3X5=O (1)	5X1=E (4)
	5X1=E (1)	19X1=S (2)	1X1=A (3)	13X1=M (1)	5X1=E (4)	
			1X1=A (2)	5X1=E (3)	3X6=R (4)	1X1=A (3)
				3X1=C (2)	2X4=H (3)	2X10=T (4)
						19X1=S (4)

			5X1=E (2)	19X1=S (2)		
		4X5=T (2)	19X1=S (1)			
		13X1=M (1)	5X1=E (2)	2X1=B (2)	2X6=L (4)	
			2X9=R (1)	2X1=B (4)	1X1=A (2)	3X5=O (4)
			5X1=E (1)	5X1=E (3)	3X3=I (2)	3X5=O (4)
		4X5=T (1)	2X10=T (3)	2X2=D (2)	3X6=R (3)	2X2=D (4)
	13X1=M (3)	5X1=E (3)				

					2X2=D (4)	
				3X5=O (4)	3X4=L (2)	
	4X5=T (1)			5X1=E (1)	2X4=H (4)	5X1=E (2)
5X1=E (1)	2X10=T (3)	1X1=A (1)	2X10=T (1)	3X6=R (1)	5X1=E (2)	4X5=T (4)
	3X1=C (3)		2X7=N (1)	3X4=L (1)	2X10=T (2)	5X1=E (4)
	5X1=E (3)	2X2=D (3)		1X1=A (1)	13X1=M (4)	19X1=S (2)
		4X5=T (3)	5X1=E (3)			

			5X5=Y (1)			
	3X4=L (2)		2X10=T (1)	2X4=H (3)	4X5=T (3)	
		1X1=A (2)	7X1=G (3)	2X7=N (1)		5X1=E (3)
	5X1=E (3)	3X3=I (3)	3X7=U (2)	5X1=E (1)	2X7=N (3)	5X1=E (3)
			2X10=T (2)		23X1=W (1)	4X5=T (1)
	2X2=D (4)	3X7=U (2)	1X1=A (4)		2X10=T (4)	
		3X6=R (4)	13X1=M (2)	3X2=F (4)		

	3X4=L (3)					
		1X1=A (3)	23X1=W (1)	5X1=E (2)	23X1=W (2)	
		3X3=I (3)	2X7=N (2)	1X1=A (1)		1X1=A (4)
	3X6=R (2)	5X1=E (2)	3X1=C (3)	7X1=G (1)	7X1=G (4)	
			5X1=E (1)	3X5=O (3)	3X3=I (4)	1X1=A (4)
			19X1=S (1)	2X7=N (4)	19X1=S (3)	

		4X4=P (3)	19X1=S (4)	3X7=U (4)		
	19X1=S (4)	5X1=E (4)	5X1=E (3)		3X4=L (4)	
			3X6=R (3)	19X1=S (2)	2X2=D (1)	2X8=P (4)
		3X2=F (3)	19X1=S (1)	2X6=L (2)	5X1=E (1)	
	5X1=E (3)	19X1=S (1)	1X1=A (2)	2X8=P (1)		
	3X1=C (3)	2X11=V (2)	5X1=E (1)	2X9=R (1)		
		4X5=T (3)	3X5=O (2)			

3X4=L (1)						
	3X3=I (1)		3X3=I (4)		3X5=O (3)	
	4X4=P (1)	2X9=R (4)		2X7=N (4)	3X7=U (3)	
	2X10=T (4)	19X1=S (1)	7X1=G (4)			4X5=T (3)
19X1=S (4)	3X1=C (1)	2X10=T (1)	5X1=E (3)	1X1=A (2)	1X1=A (3)	3X6=R (3)
	3X3=I (1)	11X1=K (1)	2X10=T (2)	7X1=G (3)	23X1=W (2)	
	2X4=H (2)	3X1=C (2)				

		3X6=R (4)	5X1=E (4)	19X1=S (1)	
		7X1=G (4)	2X9=R (1)		2X4=H (1)
	2X9=R (4)	5X1=E (1)			1X1=A (1)
	3X7=U (4)	3X8=X (2)	2X10=T (1)	4X5=T (1)	
	5X1=E (2)	2X1=B (4)	3X5=O (2)		
	19X1=S (2)	2X2=D (3)	5X1=E (3)	3X2=F (2)	1X1=A (3)
			3X3=I (3)	2X1=B (3)	

		2X10=T (4)		2X9=R (3)	
		7X1=G (2)	3X3=I (4)	5X1=E (3)	
		1X1=A (2)	1X1=A (4)		3X3=I (3)
		2X9=R (4)	2X7=N (2)	2X10=T (1)	2X8=P (3)
	4X5=T (4)	5X1=E (1)	7X1=G (2)	4X4=P (3)	2X7=N (1)
	19X1=S (1)	19X1=S (2)	7X1=G (1)	1X1=A (3)	5X1=E (1)
				13X1=M (1)	2X4=H (3)

PAGE 81

						2X10=T (1)
		2X7=N (2)			3X3=I (1)	
	3X3=I (2)	5X1=E (3)	2X2=D (2)	19X1=S (3)	3X1=C (1)	2X9=R (4)
	3X4=L (3)	3X6=R (2)	19X1=S (3)	2X4=H (4)	5X1=E (4)	11X1=K (1)
	2X8=P (3)	7X1=G (2)			4X5=T (4)	3X4=L (1)
		3X5=O (3)			5X1=E (1)	1X1=A (4)
			2X10=T (3)		3X2=F (4)	

PAGE 82

		2X1=B (1)	3X1=C (4)	11X1=K (4)		18X1=R (3)
	3X7=U (1)	1X1=A (4)	2X7=N (3)	7X1=G (3)	5X1=E (3)	
	3X1=C (1)		13X1=M (4)		3X3=I (3)	
	5X1=E (1)	11X1=K (1)		19X1=S (4)		
	4X4=P (2)	3X4=L (1)			2X4=H (2)	19X1=S (2)
		13X1=M (2)	3X3=I (2)	2X9=R (2)		

	5X1=E (2)	2X5=J (1)				
		3X3=I (2)	5X1=E (1)			
	2X4=H (2)	2X9=R (1)				
	11X1=K (1)	2X10=T (2)	3X5=O (2)	5X1=E (4)		
	5X5=Y (1)	1X1=A (4)	3X1=C (4)	3X5=O (2)	19X1=S (4)	
	2X9=R (4)	3X5=O (3)	3X3=I (3)	13X1=M (2)	1X1=A (3)	2X7=N (3)
	2X7=N (3)	2X1=B (4)	19X1=S (2)	4X5=T (3)		

	2X8=P (3)					
	19X1=S (4)	1X1=A (3)			2X2=D (2)	
	5X1=E (4)	2X7=N (3)	4X5=T (1)	19X1=S (1)	5X1=E (2)	
3X1=C (4)	2X10=T (3)	2X6=L (1)		5X1=E (2)	5X1=E (1)	
3X3=I (4)	19X1=S (3)	5X1=E (1)	3X4=L (2)		2X9=R (1)	
3X5=O (4)				2X1=B (2)		23X1=W (1)
	2X11=V (4)					

PAGE 85

			3X2=F (4)			19X1=S (4)
			3X6=R (4)	2X10=T (1)	3X3=I (4)	4X5=T (4)
		7X1=G (3)		3X7=U (4)	5X1=E (1)	
			2X9=R (3)		5X1=E (1)	19X1=S (3)
	3X6=R (2)		1X1=A (3)	3X4=L (1)	5X1=E (3)	
19X1=S (2)		3X3=I (2)		4X4=P (3)	19X1=S (1)	
	3X6=R (2)	5X1=E (2)	2X11=V (2)			

PAGE 86

			3X4=L (2)	7X1=G (1)		
		5X1=E (2)	2X7=N (1)			19X1=S (3)
	3X3=I (4)	2X11=V (2)	3X3=I (1)		2X10=T (3)	
	2X2=D (4)	5X5=Y (1)	1X1=A (2)	3X7=U (3)		
	2X9=R (1)	3X3=I (4)	4X4=P (3)	2X9=R (2)	7X1=G (2)	
3X1=C (4)		3X1=C (1)	3X5=O (4)	3X3=I (3)		
	3X3=I (4)	4X5=T (4)		2X2=D (3)		

PAGE 87

						19X1=S (1)
			4X5=T (3)		3X7=U (1)	
5X1=E (1)		2X4=H (3)		2X7=N (1)		
	2X7=N (1)		3X3=I (3)	19X1=S (1)		
2X9=R (2)		3X3=I (1)	2X4=H (1)	2X7=N (3)	11X1=K (3)	1X1=A (4)
	3X5=O (2)	3X6=R (4)	1X1=A (4)	1X1=A (2)	4X4=P (2)	13X1=M (4)
	7X1=G (4)	2X10=T (2)	19X1=S (2)	2X7=N (4)	2X2=D (4)	

PAGE 88

	1X1=A (1)			2X9=R (2)		
5X1=E (1)	2X10=T (1)			7X1=G (2)	5X1=E (2)	
	2X7=N (1)	2X4=H (1)	7X1=G (2)			4X5=T (3)
	5X1=E (1)		3X3=I (2)		3X6=R (3)	
2X1=B (1)			7X1=G (4)	2X9=R (2)	2X10=T (2)	5X1=E (3)
		3X3=I (4)	3X1=C (3)	2X9=R (4)	3X3=I (4)	3X1=C (3)
	2X7=N (4)			3X5=O (3)	2X7=N (3)	2X11=V (4)

PAGE 89

1X1=A (1)						
	2X8=P (1)	2X10=T (2)	2X9=R (1)			
5X1=E (4)	3X5=O (2)	4X4=P (1)	2X1=B (2)	3X5=O (1)	4X5=T (3)	
3X5=O (2)	2X11=V (4)	1X1=A (2)		2X9=R (3)	2X11=V (1)	
3X2=F (2)	5X1=E (4)	3X4=L (2)	3X5=O (3)	5X1=E (1)		
		2X7=N (4)	2X6=L (2)	4X4=P (3)		
		4X5=T (4)	19X1=S (4)		19X1=S (3)	

PAGE 90

	2X1=B (4)			3X6=R (1)			
	3X4=L (4)		5X1=E (1)				
		1X1=A (4)	19X1=S (1)			19X1=S (3)	2X11=V (2)
		19X1=S (1)	3X1=C (4)			1X1=A (2)	5X1=E (3)
		11X1=K (4)	5X1=E (1)	19X1=S (2)	2X10=T (3)		19X1=S (2)
				3X6=R (1)	5X1=E (2)	1X1=A (3)	
				2X2=D (1)		7X1=G (3)	

159

		5X1=E (4)	2X4=H (4)	19X1=S (4)		2X1=B (4)
	19X1=S (4)	3X2=F (3)	3X3=I (3)	3X4=L (1)	3X7=U (4)	
			5X1=E (1)	19X1=S (3)	3X2=F (1)	
			19X1=S (1)	2X4=H (3)	3X3=I (1)	
	17X1=Q (2)	19X1=S (3)	5X1=E (3)	19X1=S (1)		
		3X7=U (2)	5X1=E (2)		2X4=H (1)	
		2X10=T (2)	3X3=I (2)			

		3X1=C (4)	2X4=H (4)		3X2=F (3)	
	4X5=T (4)	2X1=B (1)	5X1=E (4)	1X1=A (3)		
	3X7=U (1)	1X1=A (4)	19X1=S (4)	11X1=K (3)		
	4X4=P (4)	3X3=I (1)	3X3=I (3)		23X1=W (2)	
	7X1=G (2)	3X4=L (1)	2X7=N (3)	3X3=I (2)		
	2X2=D (1)	2X7=N (2)	3X3=I (2)	7X1=G (3)	2X6=L (2)	
				2X6=L (2)		

		7X1=G (3)	2X7=N (3)				
	13X1=M (4)	5X1=E (2)	2X6=L (2)	3X3=I (3)	7X1=G (1)		
	3X3=I (4)		7X1=G (2)	2X10=T (3)	3X5=O (1)		
3X4=L (4)	2X7=N (1)	5X1=E (1)	2X7=N (2)	3X4=L (1)	19X1=S (3)	2X4=H (3)	
	5X1=E (4)	1X1=A (2)	2X2=D (1)		3X5=O (3)		
	1X1=A (4)		3X3=I (2)	2X9=R (2)	4X5=T (2)		
		7X1=G (4)	5X1=E (4)				

	2X8=P (4)						19X1=S (2)
	3X4=L (4)						3X3=I (2)
	5X1=E (4)	5X1=E (2)	3X4=L (2)	5X1=E (4)	2X7=N (2)		
		1X1=A (4)		7X1=G (2)	2X9=R (4)		
		2X1=B (3)	19X1=S (4)	3X7=U (4)			
	7X1=G (1)	5X5=Y (3)	2X7=N (1)	19X1=S (1)			19X1=S (3)
	3X5=O (1)	23X1=W (1)	4X4=P (3)	1X1=A (3)	19X1=S (3)		

		5X1=E (2)				
	2X10=T (2)		13X1=M (2)		2X4=H (1)	3X1=C (1)
2X9=R (4)	19X1=S (2)				5X1=E (1)	
	5X1=E (4)	5X5=Y (2)		1X1=A (1)		
5X1=E (3)	2X1=B (4)	19X1=S (2)			2X10=T (1)	
3X4=L (3)	4X4=P (3)	13X1=M (4)	5X1=E (3)		5X1=E (1)	
		4X6=X (3)	3X7=U (4)	2X7=N (4)		3X6=R (1)

	4X5=T (1)	2X7=N (1)			5X5=Y (4)	
5X1=E (3)	5X1=E (1)	3X4=L (2)	5X5=Y (2)	3X5=O (4)		
19X1=S (3)	3X6=R (2)	2X2=D (1)		2X6=L (4)	19X1=S (1)	
1X1=A (2)	1X1=A (3)	5X1=E (3)	3X7=U (1)	2X10=T (1)	4X4=P (4)	
5X1=E (2)		3X6=R (3)			13X1=M (4)	
5X5=Y (2)	3X1=C (3)				5X1=E (4)	
		2X7=N (3)	3X3=I (3)			

7X1=G (1)						
1X1=A (1)	5X5=Y (2)					
	2X9=R (1)	2X9=R (2)		2X4=H (1)		2X4=H (3)
	2X7=N (1)	3X4=L (2)	19X1=S (1)		3X1=C (3)	2X5=J (2)
		3X3=I (1)	5X1=E (2)	23X1=W (2)	5X1=E (2)	2X10=T (3)
	3X3=I (4)	2X2=D (4)		2X7=N (4)	7X1=G (4)	3X5=O (3)
	2X7=N (4)	3X2=F (4)	3X3=I (4)		2X7=N (3)	

			3X4=L (3)	19X1=S (3)		
	2X7=N (1)	3X5=O (3)		19X1=S (3)		
3X5=O (1)	3X5=O (3)	2X4=H (3)	3X1=C (3)	3X4=L (4)	2X6=L (2)	
13X1=M (1)		3X1=C (1)		5X1=E (4)	1X1=A (2)	
13X1=M (1)	3X5=O (1)		5X1=E (2)	4X5=T (2)	2X10=T (4)	3X1=C (2)
		3X1=C (2)			3X3=I (2)	2X7=N (4)
			2X4=H (2)	2X7=N (2)	1X1=A (4)	13X1=M (4)

PAGE 99

		2X4=H (1)			
	2X10=T (1)	3X6=R (3)	1X1=A (3)	5X1=E (4)	
	2X2=D (3)	2X9=R (1)	7X1=G (4)	5X1=E (3)	
		3X3=I (1)	19X1=S (2)	1X1=A (4)	2X1=B (3)
	3X1=C (2)	4X5=T (2)	2X1=B (1)	2X9=R (4)	
		5X1=E (2)	3X5=O (4)		5X1=E (2)
	19X1=S (4)	4X5=T (4)	3X2=F (2)	3X2=F (2)	

PAGE 100

3X3=I (2)					2X7=N (3)	
	2X7=N (2)			3X5=O (3)	13X1=M (4)	
	2X7=N (2)	2X4=H (1)	3X4=L (1)	3X3=I (3)		3X6=R (4)
	3X1=C (1)	3X5=O (2)	19X1=S (3)	1X1=A (1)		3X5=O (4)
	3X3=I (1)	19X1=S (3)	2X11=V (2)	2X7=N (1)	3X2=F (4)	
2X9=R (1)	5X1=E (3)	1X1=A (2)		2X7=N (4)	2X2=D (1)	
	19X1=S (3)	2X10=T (2)	5X1=E (2)	3X3=I (4)		

PAGE 101

			5X5=Y (3)			
				13X2=Z (3)	19X1=S (4)	
		3X1=C (1)	1X1=A (3)		2X7=N (2)	2X9=R (4)
	3X1=C (3)	2X9=R (3)	5X1=E (1)	2X7=N (2)	3X3=I (2)	5X1=E (4)
		5X5=Y (2)	2X7=N (1)	5X1=E (2)		23X1=W (4)
		2X10=T (1)	4X5=T (2)	3X2=F (4)	3X4=L (1)	3X5=O (4)
			2X9=R (1)	1X1=A (1)	3X4=L (4)	

PAGE 102

		2X9=R (3)			5X1=E (4)	
	2X11=V (2)		5X1=E (3)	2X8=P (4)		2X2=D (4)
	1X1=A (2)	3X3=I (4)	4X4=P (4)	4X5=T (3)		
	2X6=L (4)	3X4=L (2)	5X1=E (2)	19X1=S (3)	3X6=R (1)	
	3X2=F (4)	19X1=S (1)	2X7=N (2)	1X1=A (1)	3X5=O (3)	4X4=P (3)
		2X10=T (2)	4X4=P (1)	13X1=M (1)		
	3X3=I (2)	2X7=N (2)	5X1=E (2)			

						5X1=E (3)
	5X1=E (1)				3X4=L (3)	
2X9=R (1)		2X10=T (1)			7X1=G (3)	
	3X1=C (4)	4X5=T (1)	3X2=F (2)	3X5=O (3)	1X1=A (2)	
3X5=O (4)	3X3=I (2)	1X1=A (2)	5X1=E (1)	3X2=F (2)	3X5=O (3)	
3X6=R (2)	3X5=O (4)		2X6=L (1)	5X1=E (4)		7X1=G (3)
		11X1=K (4)	3X3=I (4)		19X1=S (4)	

			3X6=R (3)		2X6=L (4)	7X1=G (4)
		19X1=S (2)	5X1=E (3)	1X1=A (4)		
	4X5=T (2)		2X7=N (3)	5X1=E (1)	13X1=M (4)	3X5=O (4)
2X11=V (1)	1X1=A (2)		2X10=T (1)	4X5=T (3)		2X9=R (4)
3X3=I (1)		5X1=E (2)	1X1=A (1)	3X1=C (2)	5X1=E (3)	
	2X1=B (1)	2X9=R (1)	3X4=L (2)		2X2=D (3)	

PAGE 105

2X9=R (3)	5X1=E (1)						
7X1=G (1)	5X1=E (3)		4X4=P (4)		19X1=S (2)		
2X8=P (3)	1X1=A (1)		3X5=O (4)		4X5=T (2)		
4X4=P (3)	7X1=G (1)	5X1=E (4)		1X1=A (2)			
2X7=N (1)	3X5=O (3)	3X1=C (3)	13X1=M (4)	2X1=B (2)			
5X1=E (1)	2X4=H (3)	19X1=S (4)	2X6=L (2)				
				5X1=E (2)			

PAGE 106

			19X1=S (2)		1X1=A (4)		
1X1=A (1)		5X1=E (2)	5X1=E (1)	3X4=L (4)		4X5=T (4)	
2X9=R (3)	23X1=W (1)	2X9=R (1)	3X3=I (2)	3X3=I (4)	5X1=E (4)		
5X1=E (3)	1X1=A (1)		2X2=D (2)		2X8=P (4)		
2X2=D (3)		3X5=O (2)					
2X7=N (3)	2X1=B (2)		2X9=R (3)	3X7=U (3)	19X1=S (3)		
	5X1=E (3)	3X6=R (3)					

PAGE 107

				2X7=N (2)		
3X1=C (1)	2X4=H (1)	19X1=S (3)	3X3=I (2)	3X5=O (4)	7X1=G (2)	
		5X1=E (1)	2X7=N (3)	13X1=M (2)	2X9=R (4)	
		3X1=C (1)	3X5=O (3)	3X1=C (4)	1X1=A (2)	
	3X6=R (1)	3X3=I (3)	11X1=K (1)	3X3=I (4)	7X1=G (2)	
	4X5=T (3)	5X1=E (1)			13X1=M (4)	
	1X1=A (3)	2X10=T (3)	19X1=S (3)			

PAGE 108

				19X1=S (4)	3X1=C (1)	
			2X10=T (1)	3X3=I (1)	2X6=L (4)	
	2X7=N (3)	19X1=S (1)			5X1=E (4)	
	1X1=A (1)	2X9=R (3)	1X1=A (2)	5X1=E (2)	5X1=E (4)	2X4=H (4)
	3X4=L (1)	3X6=R (2)	3X7=U (3)		2X4=H (2)	
	2X10=T (2)	4X4=P (1)	2X1=B (3)			

		2X6=L (2)				
	1X1=A (2)				7X1=G (1)	
		3X7=U (2)		2X1=B (4)	3X4=L (1)	
2X9=R (3)	3X8=X (2)		5X1=E (4)	3X5=O (1)	3X6=R (4)	
5X1=E (2)	3X5=O (3)	13X1=M (3)	13X2=Z (4)	19X1=S (1)	5X1=E (4)	
	19X1=S (2)	3X6=R (3)		5X1=E (4)	19X1=S (1)	
			1X1=A (3)		5X5=Y (1)	

PAGE 110

	19X1=S (2)				5X1=E (3)	
	1X1=A (2)			19X1=S (3)	19X1=S (3)	
13X1=M (4)		2X2=D (2)		3X6=R (3)		
	2X9=R (4)	2X2=D (2)	23X1=W (1)	5X1=E (2)	3X5=O (3)	
	3X5=O (4)	2X9=R (1)	3X4=L (2)		2X4=H (3)	
11X1=K (1)	3X2=F (4)	5X1=E (1)				
	3X1=C (1)	3X3=I (4)	2X7=N (4)	3X7=U (4)		

				3X3=I (3)	19X1=S (3)	
		4X4=P (1)	3X7=U (3)			5X1=E (3)
		5X1=E (1)		3X6=R (3)	3X1=C (3)	
	19X1=S (2)		2X2=D (1)			
19X1=S (4)		2X9=R (2)	1X1=A (1)		1X1=A (4)	4X4=P (4)
	3X6=R (4)	3X4=L (1)	5X1=E (2)	13X1=M (4)	2X1=B (2)	
		5X1=E (4)	4X4=P (4)	11X1=K (2)	3X3=I (2)	

	5X1=E (3)					
2X10=T (3)	23X1=W (3)	3X5=O (1)				
3X3=I (3)	5X1=E (3)		2X9=R (1)			2X8=P (4)
19X1=S (3)	2X1=B (3)		7X1=G (1)		3X3=I (4)	
		1X1=A (1)	5X1=E (4)	3X1=C (4)		
3X4=L (2)		2X9=R (4)	2X7=N (1)	11X1=K (4)	19X1=S (2)	
	1X1=A (2)	2X9=R (2)	3X3=I (2)	2X8=P (2)		

PAGE 113

	4X4=P (2)	19X1=S (4)	7X1=G (2)	3X3=I (4)	5X1=E (4)	
	1X1=A (2)		3X1=C (4)	2X7=N (2)		2X7=N (4)
	2X9=R (2)	3X1=C (1)	3X3=I (2)	19X1=S (3)	3X6=R (1)	3X1=C (4)
	2X4=H (1)	2X10=T (2)	2X6=L (3)	5X1=E (1)	5X1=E (4)	
	1X1=A (1)		3X4=L (3)	3X1=C (1)	2X10=T (1)	
		2X9=R (1)	1X1=A (1)	5X1=E (3)		
					3X1=C (3)	

PAGE 114

	19X1=S (3)					
5X1=E (3)	19X1=S (1)	2X1=B (3)	2X1=B (3)	5X1=E (3)		
	3X4=L (3)	3X1=C (1)			2X8=P (3)	
		5X1=E (1)		2X2=D (4)		
	2X7=N (1)	4X4=P (2)	19X1=S (1)		5X1=E (4)	
		5X1=E (1)	19X1=S (2)	2X6=L (4)	3X1=C (2)	1X1=A (4)
			3X3=I (2)	2X9=R (2)	2X1=B (4)	

PAGE 115

		2X2=D (4)	5X1=E (3)	2X9=R (4)			
	5X1=E (4)		3X7=U (4)	3X1=C (3)			5X1=E (1)
	3X1=C (4)		4X5=T (4)	3X5=O (3)			3X1=C (1)
	19X1=S (2)	1X1=A (4)	3X2=F (1)	2X7=N (3)	1X1=A (1)		
		2X10=T (2)	3X7=U (1)	3X5=O (3)	2X7=N (1)		
		3X6=R (2)	13X1=M (3)	2X9=R (1)			
	1X1=A (2)	23X1=W (2)		5X5=Y (3)			

PAGE 116

		2X9=R (2)	3X1=C (3)	2X10=T (3)			
	5X1=E (2)	3X3=I (3)	1X1=A (2)	3X4=L (2)	5X1=E (4)		
	2X9=R (3)	13X1=M (2)		4X5=T (4)	3X2=F (2)		
		2X10=T (3)	19X1=S (3)	3X3=I (3)	1X1=A (4)		
		3X3=I (1)	2X11=V (1)	2X6=L (4)	2X2=D (3)		
	3X4=L (1)	7X1=G (1)		3X5=O (4)			
	5X1=E (1)	2X6=L (1)	1X1=A (1)			19X1=S (4)	3X3=I (4)